AGE OF KNOWING

THE PSYCHIC EVOLUTION OF THE HUMAN RACE

Tina Ketch

AGE OF KNOWING
THE PSYCHIC EVOLUTION OF THE HUMAN RACE

ISBN: 979-8-9931385-8-9
eISBN: 979-8-9931385-9-6

For information, inquiries, or permissions, contact:
https://TinaKetch.com
TinaKetch@me.com
https://YouTube.com/TinaKetch

DEDICATION

To the awakened, the awakening, and the ones who have yet to remember, you are all part of the same light.

- Tina Ketch

EPIGRAPHS

"We are not human beings having a spiritual experience.

We are spiritual beings having a human experience."

- Pierre Teilhard de Chardin

"We are entering the age where belief is no longer enough; we must become what we know."

- Tina Ketch

TABLE OF CONTENTS

FOREWORD

The Moment of Remembering

Every generation believes it is living in extraordinary times. Yet what we are experiencing now transcends any previous era of transformation. We are not merely advancing technologically or philosophically; we are shifting vibrationally. The pulse of the Earth is changing, and with it, every living being is being called to awaken to a greater dimension of awareness.

For centuries, humanity has looked to the stars, scriptures, and laboratories for answers to life's greatest questions. Who are we? Why are we here? What happens beyond what we can see? The answers have always been available, but the human mind, conditioned by fear and separation, has only been able to perceive fragments of the truth. Today, those fragments are coming together. We are beginning to perceive the full spectrum of what it means to be alive.

This book, Age of Knowing: The Psychic Evolution of the Human Race, is written at the threshold of a new consciousness. It does not offer prediction or persuasion, but illumination. It speaks to the logical mind and the intuitive heart alike, reminding both that they were never meant to be in conflict; they are complementary instruments of a single awareness.

In this age, intuition is emerging as the next step in human evolution. No longer the realm of mystics alone, intuition is becoming a universal language, an intelligence that integrates sensory data, emotional awareness, and energetic communication. It enables us to understand what words cannot express and to recognize patterns that extend far beyond linear logic. Humanity is awakening not because of belief, but because of biology. The human system, neural, cellular, and energetic, is adapting to higher frequencies of existence.

The Science and Spirit of Change

Science has begun to touch the edges of this truth. The discovery that thoughts and emotions influence the molecular structure of water, that energy fields surround and sustain every organism, and that consciousness itself may be the foundation of physical reality, all point toward one conclusion: we are participants in creation, not its bystanders.

The Earth, too, is evolving. Her resonance is rising, her cycles accelerating. Geophysical and electromagnetic shifts mirror the emotional and psychological upheavals within humanity. As above, so below; as within, so without. What we witness in the world, the polarization, the unrest, the hunger for meaning, is not chaos but the birth of coherence. Old systems are collapsing, not because the world is ending, but because consciousness is beginning.

This book is written for those who feel the tremors of that change within themselves, those who sense that something profound is occurring beneath the surface of ordinary life. It is for the thinkers who have glimpsed intuition, and the intuitives who have sought understanding. It is for those who know that science and spirit are not opposites but two expressions of the same truth.

The Return of Inner Authority

Institutions or doctrines will not lead humanity's next great awakening. It will rise from within each individual who reclaims their capacity to know. The era of blind belief is coming to an end; the era of conscious knowing has begun. To know is not to assume superiority; it is to accept responsibility. Awareness demands participation. Once you understand that thought, emotion, and intention shape reality, you can no longer live unconsciously. You become a creator by design rather than by default.

Psychic development is not a fringe pursuit in this new age; it is the natural evolution of perception. The word *"psychic"* means *"of the soul.* " To develop one's psychic awareness is to awaken the soul's sensory system, to perceive the invisible architecture of life that has always been there. What was once considered supernatural will soon be understood as natural.

A Planetary Invitation

This work serves as both a guidebook and a mirror, reflecting the transformation already underway within every human heart. It offers clarity where confusion reigns, and empowerment where fear has taken hold. It reminds us that awakening is not escape; it is engagement. It is the conscious realization that the Earth is not a resource to be used but a being to be harmonized with.

Each page invites the reader to approach truth not through dogma, but through direct experience, to test, feel, and observe. In this way, Age of Knowing becomes more than a book; it becomes a process of initiation. The reader does not simply absorb information; they begin to awaken through it.

The Bridge Between Worlds

Tina Ketch has long been a messenger between worlds, blending spiritual insight with grounded intelligence, ancient wisdom with contemporary relevance. Her writing demystifies the unseen without diminishing its sacredness. In this work, she steps fully into the role of translator of the new consciousness, guiding readers through the evolving interface between Earth's energetic shift and the expansion of human potential.

This foreword, therefore, is not just an introduction; it is an acknowledgment of arrival. We have reached the point where the mystical and the measurable converge, where energy meets evidence, and where humanity begins to perceive itself as part of a conscious universe.

The Threshold of Knowing

The Age of Knowing is not a prophecy of what will come; it is a recognition of what already is. We are awakening into a multidimensional reality, remembering that every thought is energy, every action vibration, and every human being a field of light capable of awareness beyond measure.

To read this book is to participate in that awakening, to begin seeing not only the world as it appears, but as it truly is: a vast network of consciousness evolving toward unity.

The time of seeking is ending. The time of knowing has begun.

PREFACE

The Age We Have Entered

Humanity stands at a threshold unlike any it has ever faced. We are not merely witnessing a societal evolution; we are experiencing an evolution of consciousness. It is subtle and immense, personal and planetary, invisible to the eye yet unmistakable to the soul.

For generations, we have looked outward for meaning, searching for proof of the unseen in science, religion, authority, and the stars. Now, we are turning inward and discovering that the universe we sought has been within us all along.

We are entering what I call the Age of Knowing, a period in human development where intuition becomes as valid as intellect, and spiritual perception joins hands with scientific understanding. It is not an age of belief, because belief requires faith without proof. It is not an age of religion, because religion divides what is sacred into doctrines and walls. It is an age of direct awareness, of knowing without doubt, sensing without fear, and understanding without intermediaries.

In this new age, truth is no longer handed down; it is awakened within. Each individual becomes both student and teacher, seeker and sage, responsible for cultivating their own inner knowing. We begin to remember that knowledge is not acquired through competition or comparison, but through communion with nature, with others, and with the deeper self that connects us all.

The Age of Knowing calls for courage, the courage to feel what we have numbed, to question what we once accepted, and to release what no longer resonates. It asks that we listen not only to the words of the wise, but to the whisper of our own soul. In this stillness, we begin to discern truth not as opinion, but as vibration, a resonance that aligns us with what is real, timeless, and whole.

This era will not be defined by technology or power, but by frequency, the unseen current of thought, emotion, and intention that shapes our shared reality. Those who learn to master this current will not dominate others; they will harmonize with the greater symphony of creation. Knowing is not about control; it is about alignment. It is living as one with the infinite intelligence that breathes through all that exists.

The Age of Knowing is the bridge between worlds, between what has been and what is becoming. It invites us to walk forward with open eyes, open minds, and open hearts, recognizing that the future is not something that happens to us, but something we are co-creating in every moment.

As the veils lift and remembrance stirs, may we each step into this new age not as followers of light, but as bearers of it, living proof that the divine has always been within us, waiting to be known.

Author's Blessing

May this book serve as a mirror to your awakening, reflecting the truth that you have always been enough, always been connected, and always been whole.

May it remind you that your knowing is sacred, your awareness is power, and your presence is light.

Walk gently, yet boldly, into this Age of Knowing.

For you are the dawn you have been waiting for.

- Tina Ketch

INTRODUCTION

A New Map of Human Potential

There was a time when human potential was measured only by intellect, strength, or survival. But a new measure is emerging, one that defies conventional understanding. It is the measure of awareness, vibration, and consciousness itself.

Every person alive today is part of a vast experiment, one not run by laboratories or governments, but by creation itself. We are being invited to evolve beyond the limits of perception, to understand that the next frontier is not outer space but inner space. The human mind, body, and soul are becoming instruments of universal intelligence, capable of interpreting information once thought beyond our reach.

Modern science has already begun to glimpse this reality. Quantum physics demonstrates that the observer influences what is observed, indicating that consciousness is an active participant in the creation process. Neuroscience shows that the human brain is capable of rewiring itself in response to experience; what we think and feel literally reshapes our biology. The study of epigenetics reveals that our environment, emotions, and intentions influence gene expression. What once seemed mystical is now measurable.

At the same time, humanity is awakening spiritually. People everywhere are reporting spontaneous intuitive insights, telepathic experiences, energy sensitivity, and profound states of connection with nature and one another. These are not anomalies; they are evidence that we are remembering who we truly are: conscious beings in communication with a conscious universe.

The psychic evolution of the human race is not about developing supernatural abilities. It is about restoring natural awareness, remembering how to sense the world beyond physical form, to interact with energy as easily as with matter, and to live as co-creators within a vibrational ecosystem.

In this book, we will explore this awakening through both lenses and languages: the measurable science of frequency and the timeless wisdom of the spirit. We will explore how Earth's shifting resonance reflects our emotional evolution, how thought and intention shape reality, and how empathy and intuition are preparing us for the next stage of civilization.

This is not theory; it is observation. The evidence of change surrounds us, in our bodies, our relationships, our environment, and our collective consciousness. The Age of Knowing is the moment when humanity stops asking if these things are real and begins to understand how they work.

The chapters that follow will reveal how the Earth is guiding us through this transition. Together, we will examine the energetic blueprint of the planet and its direct relationship with the human energy field, because to understand humanity's evolution, we must first understand the Conscious Planet that is carrying us into the future.

PART I: THE AWAKENING EARTH

Earth is a conscious being whose rhythms and cycles guide human transformation. This part explores how planetary changes awaken humanity's deeper perception.

CHAPTER ONE

THE CONSCIOUS PLANET

The Earth as a Living Being

The Earth is not a rock suspended in space; it is a living organism. Beneath her mountains, within her oceans, and through every breath of wind moves an intelligent rhythm that sustains all life. Ancient civilizations understood this truth instinctively. They named her Gaia, Pachamama, and Danu, not as metaphors, but as acknowledgment of an aware and responsive being. The Earth breathes, feels, and communicates. Her body is the landscape; her pulse, the resonance that echoes through every living system.

For most of modern history, science has regarded the planet as inert matter, driven by mechanical forces and geological chance. Yet, the deeper science peers into the fabric of reality, the more it encounters something extraordinary: pattern, precision, and purpose. From the oscillation of atomic fields to the geometry of galaxies, the universe behaves like a vast, interconnected organism, and the Earth is one of its conscious cells.

The Gaia Hypothesis: Science Meets Spirit

In the 1970s, atmospheric chemist James Lovelock and microbiologist Lynn Margulis proposed the Gaia Hypothesis, a revolutionary idea that the Earth regulates itself like a living organism. They observed that the planet maintains a delicate balance of temperature, oxygen, salinity, and chemical composition, all of which are fine-tuned to support life.

Lovelock wrote, *"The entire range of living matter on Earth, from whales to viruses, and from oaks to algae, could be regarded as constituting a single living entity."*

Though radical at the time, his concept now finds resonance across multiple scientific disciplines, ecology, systems theory, and quantum biology. The Earth functions as a self-regulating, dynamic system: an intelligent feedback loop between life and environment. The biosphere, atmosphere, hydrosphere, and lithosphere are not separate layers but organs of one vast being, Gaia.

To the spiritually aware, this is not new knowledge but a scientific rediscovery of ancient wisdom. Indigenous traditions worldwide have long perceived the Earth as a conscious entity, a mother, a teacher, and a mirror of human behavior. When humanity harms the Earth, we are wounding our own extended body.

The Schumann Resonance: The Earth's Pulse

Every living organism has a heartbeat, and so does the Earth. In 1952, physicist Winfried Otto Schumann mathematically predicted that electromagnetic waves continuously resonate in the space between the Earth's surface and the ionosphere. This global frequency, now known as the Schumann Resonance, averages around 7.83 hertz, within the same range as the human brain's alpha waves, which are associated with calmness, intuition, and meditative awareness.

This resonance is not merely a scientific curiosity; it is a bridge between human biology and planetary consciousness. When we relax, meditate, or feel grounded, our brain waves synchronize with the Earth's natural rhythm. When global events generate fear, chaos, or emotional upheaval, measurable spikes in the planet's electromagnetic activity occur. Humanity and the Earth are locked in a constant energetic conversation, a two-way feedback loop of frequency and feeling.

Recent monitoring has shown that the amplitude of the Schumann Resonance is increasing, sometimes surging far beyond traditional baselines. Many researchers and intuitives interpret this as evidence of a planetary frequency shift, the Earth *"accelerating"* as consciousness itself expands.

Whether viewed scientifically or spiritually, the implication is profound: the planet and her people are evolving together.

The Language of Energy

Energy is the invisible language through which the Earth communicates. Every vibration, whether seismic, emotional, or electromagnetic, carries information. Trees translate sunlight into sugars, oceans translate moonlight into tides, and humans translate vibration into thought and feeling.

This exchange forms a unified field of intelligence. The magnetic field surrounding the planet acts as both shield and transmitter, carrying data between the Earth and the cosmos. Solar flares, cosmic rays, and galactic radiation continually bathe this field, influencing not only weather patterns but consciousness itself.

When solar activity intensifies, people often report experiencing heightened emotions, insomnia, vivid dreams, or spiritual insights. These experiences are not random; they reflect the body's sensitivity to shifts in the planet's energetic environment. The human nervous system, like an antenna, responds to the Earth's electrical and magnetic changes.

Modern instruments can measure these effects, yet the heart and intuition have always felt them. Indigenous timekeepers observed such cycles centuries ago, linking human mood, fertility, and even conflict to the rhythm of the Sun and Earth. The ancients lived in attunement with Gaia's subtle cues; modern humanity is rediscovering how.

The Planetary Nervous System

If we view the planet as a living organism, its ecosystems become its organs, and its energy lines, the ley lines and magnetic meridians, function like a nervous system. These lines distribute energetic information, connecting sacred sites such as the Pyramids of Giza, Stonehenge, Machu Picchu, and Uluru in geometric harmony.

Modern mapping reveals that many ancient temples align perfectly with intersections of these energetic currents, suggesting that early civilizations were consciously harmonizing with the Earth's natural energy grid. They understood that to build in resonance with Gaia was to live in harmony with creation.

Just as the human body's acupuncture points regulate vitality, these planetary nodes regulate the Earth's vibrational health. When the energy flow of the planet is blocked, through destruction, pollution, or imbalance, it weakens, and humanity experiences corresponding disharmony, including physical illness, emotional unrest, and environmental crises.

The global awakening we are witnessing today is, in essence, the activation of the Earth's nervous system. The rise in human empathy, sensitivity, and psychic awareness mirrors the reactivation of these planetary meridians. The Earth is transmitting at a higher frequency, and the human collective is tuning in.

Gaia and the Collective Field

Every human thought, emotion, and action contributes to the planet's energetic environment. This is not a metaphor; it is a measurable phenomenon. The Global Consciousness Project at Princeton University demonstrated that random number generators around the world display measurable coherence during moments of global unity or tragedy. Consciousness itself influences physical systems.

The Earth responds to our coherence. When millions of people meditate, pray, or focus on compassion, measurable harmony appears in the global electromagnetic field. When fear dominates, the field becomes turbulent. We are not separate from Gaia; we are neurons in her planetary brain.

This symbiosis means that caring for the Earth is not charity; it is self-preservation. Pollution, greed, and conflict disrupt not only the physical environment but also the collective energy grid. Healing the planet begins with healing the human mind and heart, for the outer world mirrors the inner state of humanity.

The Awakening Partnership

The concept of Earth as conscious does not diminish humanity's role; it elevates it. We are not accidents of biology but expressions of planetary intelligence. The minerals in our bones come from her crust, the salt in our blood from her oceans, the breath in our lungs from her trees. Our consciousness is the Earth's awareness looking back at itself.

This partnership is now reaching a new stage of maturity. Just as a child eventually recognizes the parent within themselves, humanity is awakening to the realization that we are co-creators with Gaia. She evolves through us, through our learning, our mistakes, our compassion, and our capacity to transform.

The Age of Knowing is the age of remembrance: the time when humanity acknowledges that every life form, every ecosystem, and every element is part of a living dialogue of creation.

When we attune to the Earth's consciousness, we find stability in chaos, peace in uncertainty, and purpose in our existence. Her pulse becomes our rhythm; her wisdom, our guide.

In Summary

- The Earth is a self-regulating, living organism with measurable intelligence and rhythm.
- The Schumann Resonance serves as the electromagnetic link between planetary and human consciousness.
- Humanity's emotional and psychic evolution mirrors Gaia's energetic ascension.
- The planetary energy grid acts as a nervous system connecting all sacred sites and consciousness centers.
- Collective intention directly influences the coherence of Earth's field, proving that awareness shapes reality.

Closing Reflection

The planet is not evolving separately from us; it is evolving through us. Each time we pause to breathe in harmony with the Earth, we contribute to her healing. Each thought of gratitude, each act of compassion, strengthens her electromagnetic heart.

As we awaken, we discover that we were never strangers on this planet; we are extensions of her consciousness, remembering what she has always known:

That all life is one field, one body, and one breath.

CHAPTER TWO

THE PULSE OF CHANGE

How the Earth Communicates Through Frequency

Every living system has a rhythm, a pulse through which it breathes, regenerates, and evolves. The Earth's pulse is measured not only in cycles of day and night, or seasons of growth and rest, but in the subtle oscillations of energy that shape consciousness itself. These rhythmic changes, solar cycles, geomagnetic shifts, and cosmic waves are not background noise; they are the living heartbeat of creation. Humanity is now learning to hear it.

The universe is not silent. From the hum of atoms to the spiral motion of galaxies, all existence vibrates in harmony with a grand symphony of frequency. The Earth, as a conscious participant in this cosmic orchestra, receives and transmits energetic information through its magnetic field. This field does not merely protect the planet; it communicates with the Sun, the stars, and all sentient life.

In times of accelerated solar activity or geomagnetic fluctuation, this dialogue intensifies. The result is what we now experience as global energetic acceleration —an invisible quickening that affects weather, emotions, and consciousness simultaneously. This is the pulse of change.

The Solar Connection

The Sun is more than a source of light; it is a transmitter of consciousness. Every solar flare, coronal mass ejection, or shift in solar wind carries electromagnetic data that reaches Earth's atmosphere within minutes and penetrates its magnetic field. These waves of energy affect not only the climate but also the electrical activity within every living being.

When solar storms occur, many people report sensations such as restlessness, insomnia, vivid dreams, emotional surges, or profound clarity. Medical studies have shown that fluctuations in geomagnetic activity can influence blood pressure, heart rhythms, and even patterns of collective behavior. But beyond biology, these changes stir something more profound, a psychic awakening within the human system.

As the Sun pulses, the human nervous system responds like a string on a cosmic instrument. We are literally tuned by light. Each burst of solar energy stimulates not just our cells but our consciousness, opening latent pathways of awareness. This is why moments of global illumination, scientific breakthroughs, spiritual awakenings, and revolutions in art and understanding often correspond with heightened solar activity. The universe itself is a teacher, and the Sun is one of its most direct messengers.

Geomagnetic Resonance and Emotional Waves

The Earth's magnetic field, known as the magnetosphere, is a vast cocoon of energy generated by the movement of molten iron in the planet's core. It serves as both a shield and a translator, mediating between cosmic radiation and biological life.

When solar winds interact with this field, they create oscillations, geomagnetic storms, that ripple across the planet. These energetic waves influence not only technology and weather patterns but also human emotion.

Scientific data have shown correlations between geomagnetic disturbances and increased hospital admissions for anxiety, mood disorders, and sleep disruption. Conversely, when the field is calm and stable, collective emotional states tend toward harmony and coherence.

These findings affirm what the mystics have long known: our emotions are not isolated; they are planetary. We are constantly exchanging energy with the Earth's field, amplifying or calming the global vibration with every thought and feeling.

When we experience internal chaos, it contributes to external turbulence. When we cultivate peace, we help stabilize the field. The Earth is not separate from our consciousness; she mirrors it, amplifies it, and responds to it.

The Cosmic Web

Beyond our solar system lies an invisible lattice of electromagnetic filaments connecting galaxies, stars, and planetary systems, a cosmic nervous system known as the Intergalactic Web. Through this web, energy and information travel as plasma streams and photonic currents. Earth's magnetic field, though localized, is sensitive to these cosmic transmissions.

Astrophysicists have begun to detect high-frequency waves and bursts of gamma radiation emanating from distant galaxies and reaching our planet. From a spiritual perspective, these are the frequency codes of evolution, signals that accelerate the evolution of consciousness. Many intuitives have described these influxes as *"light downloads,"* moments when new understanding or awareness floods the mind seemingly from nowhere.

The correlation between these cosmic events and humanity's spiritual growth is more than a poetic coincidence. As the planet's resonance rises, it becomes capable of receiving and decoding these higher-frequency messages. What once felt like inspiration may, in truth, be the universe communicating through resonance.

The cosmic web is the nervous system of creation, and Earth, through her magnetosphere, is one of its living receptors.

The Rhythms of the Ages

Throughout history, civilizations have risen and fallen in cycles corresponding to astronomical alignments and energetic shifts. The Mayans, Egyptians, Vedic sages, and other ancient astronomers tracked these long-term patterns, understanding that time itself is not linear but vibrational, a spiral of ascending and descending frequency.

We are now transitioning between these great cycles, moving from the density of the Age of Unknowing into the illumination of the Age of Knowing. In astrological terms, this correlates with the shift into the Age of Aquarius, symbolizing higher communication, collective intelligence, and unity consciousness.

This is not superstition; it is the natural progression of cosmic resonance. Every few thousand years, the solar system passes through new regions of the galaxy, each with its own energetic properties. As the heliosphere encounters these fields, the frequency of sunlight and magnetism subtly changes, influencing life on Earth. Evolution itself is not random mutation; it is resonance adaptation.

Humanity evolves because the planet grows, and the planet evolves because the cosmos evolves. Everything breathes in sync.

The Human Response to Planetary Change

Our bodies are exquisitely tuned to the Earth's electromagnetic field. The heart, brain, and DNA act as receivers and amplifiers of planetary signals. When the Earth's frequency shifts, we feel it, physically, emotionally, and spiritually.

Everyday experiences during energetic shifts may include:

- Fatigue or restlessness as the nervous system recalibrates.
- Emotional sensitivity or spontaneous empathy.
- Heightened intuition or psychic awareness.

- Vivid dreams, synchronicities, and déjà vu experiences.
- A desire to simplify, release, and reconnect with nature.

These are not symptoms of illness; they are signs of attunement. The human instrument is being tuned to a higher octave of consciousness. Just as a radio must adjust its dial to receive a clearer signal, we are learning to align our energy with the planet's evolving vibration.

This adjustment period can feel unstable, as the old frequencies within us, fear, anger, and separation, rise to the surface for release. But beneath the discomfort lies a powerful truth: humanity is adapting to live in resonance with the planet's ascension.

Coherence: The Key to Stability

The most effective way to navigate this energetic acceleration is through coherence, which involves aligning the heart, mind, and body with the Earth's natural rhythm. When we are coherent, we become stable conduits of energy rather than chaotic transmitters.

Practices such as meditation, conscious breathing, sound healing, and time spent in nature restore coherence within the body's electromagnetic field. Studies show that when large groups enter this state simultaneously, measurable harmony appears in global geomagnetic data. This means that personal peace contributes to planetary stability, a literal truth, not a metaphor.

The Earth's pulse grows stronger when ours is steady.

The New Science of Synchronization

Emerging research in fields such as neurocardiology, quantum biology, and biofield science supports what spiritual traditions have taught for millennia: everything is connected through vibration.

- The HeartMath Institute has demonstrated that the human heart synchronizes with the Earth's magnetic field, and that emotional coherence can influence this connection.
- The Global Coherence Monitoring System measures correlations between collective human emotion and fluctuations in geomagnetic activity.
- Quantum coherence studies show that biological systems maintain order through wave resonance rather than chemical reaction alone.

The implication is profound: consciousness is a planetary force. Our emotions, thoughts, and collective state of awareness are not confined to the individual; they radiate into the energetic environment, shaping the very fabric of reality.

The universe does not evolve around us; it evolves through us.

The Great Alignment

As the Earth continues to align with higher-frequency currents of cosmic energy, humanity stands at the threshold of a remarkable opportunity: to consciously participate in its own evolution. The pulse of change is not something to endure but something to join.

Each act of compassion, each moment of inner stillness, and each decision made from love rather than fear harmonizes the human field with the planetary field. This is how we co-create with Gaia, not through control, but through resonance.

When enough individuals achieve coherence, the collective vibration reaches a tipping point, a phase shift in consciousness. History records these moments as renaissances, awakenings, and golden ages. Spiritually, they are the planet's heartbeat quickening as she ascends to her next octave of being.

In Summary

- Solar and geomagnetic activity act as catalysts for human and planetary evolution.
- The Earth's magnetosphere is a dynamic, conscious field that mirrors collective emotion.
- Cosmic radiation and solar influxes influence biological and psychic processes.
- Coherence within the individual contributes to coherence within the planet.
- Humanity's awakening is synchronized with the rhythmic pulse of the universe.

Closing Reflection

The pulse of the Earth is the pulse of your own heart. When you feel restless, exhausted, or inspired beyond reason, remember, the planet is speaking. Her magnetic tides flow through your bloodstream. Her resonance hums in your cells. Her evolution is your evolution.

In learning to listen to her pulse, you rediscover your own rhythm within creation. The heartbeat of the Earth and the heartbeat of humanity are one, and together, they are preparing for a new symphony of consciousness.

CHAPTER THREE

THE CYCLES OF ASCENSION

The Rhythm of Creation

Everything in existence moves in circles. Stars spiral around their galactic centers, the Earth spins through day and night, and every cell in the human body pulses with periodic life. Nothing in nature travels in a straight line; it curves, returns, repeats, refines. This looping rhythm, birth, expansion, contraction, renewal, is the fingerprint of divine intelligence written into the structure of time itself.

Evolution, then, is not a climb up a ladder but a spiral through dimensions of awareness. Each revolution elevates consciousness to a higher octave of understanding, revisiting familiar themes on a broader scale. These spirals, cosmic, planetary, and human, are the cycles of ascension.

The Music of Time

Physics tells us that time is not a river flowing forward but a frequency that oscillates. Ancient mystics called it the *"music of the spheres,"* the harmonics through which creation measures itself. When energy repeats at intervals, it generates stability, memory, and growth.

Our solar system, too, vibrates in harmonic patterns. Every orbit, every rotation, every magnetic reversal acts as a beat within the cosmic symphony. These movements are not random mechanics; they are instructions for consciousness, signatures of evolution encoded in motion.

Planetary Rhythms and Celestial Clockwork

One of the grandest of these patterns is the precession of the equinoxes, the slow wobble of Earth's axis that completes a circle every 25,920 years. As the axis shifts, the backdrop of constellations behind the rising Sun on the spring equinox changes, ushering humanity through twelve astronomical *"Ages."* Each Age, approximately 2,160 years long, carries a distinct energetic theme that shapes culture, belief, and awareness.

- The **Age of Taurus** (approx. 4300–2150 BCE) centered on material mastery and fertility, hence the bull-gods of Egypt and Mesopotamia.
- The **Age of Aries** birthed conquest and willpower, symbolized by the ram and the rise of empires.
- The **Age of Pisces** emphasized faith, sacrifice, and devotion, its symbol the fish.
- The **Age of Aquarius**, dawning now, heralds knowledge, cooperation, and unity through consciousness and technology.

Precession is the cosmic pendulum of awareness. As the Earth tilts, the psyche of humanity tilts with it.

Beyond precession, shorter solar cycles occur roughly every 11 years as the Sun's magnetic poles reverse. These solar maxima and minima bathe Earth in waves of charged particles that subtly affect weather patterns, electromagnetic resonance, and even collective mood. During solar peaks, creativity, discovery, and restlessness surge; during quiet phases, humanity integrates and consolidates.

Larger geomagnetic and galactic cycles, about 26,000, 52,000, and 104,000 years, mark deeper pulses of transformation, when solar radiation, cosmic rays, and gravitational alignments open gateways of accelerated evolution. These cycles correspond with geological upheavals, mass extinctions, and cultural renaissances, the universe's way of resetting the field for new consciousness.

Ancient Calendars of Light

Long before telescopes, ancient civilizations mapped these rhythms with astonishing precision.

The **Mayan Long Count Calendar** tracks a 5,125-year epoch nested within the greater precessional cycle. To the Maya, time was not linear but alive, a breathing deity. The completion of the last cycle in 2012 was never an *"end of the world,"* but the closing of one vibrational octave and the opening of another, an invitation for humanity to awaken to conscious participation.

The **Egyptian Zep Tepi**, the *"First Time,"* described epochs when the gods walked among men, periods of heightened resonance when Earth's vibration allowed direct communication between planes. The ancient Hindus encoded a similar understanding in the Yugas, vast cycles of spiritual rise and decline, culminating in the Satya Yuga, or the Age of Truth. Each tradition recognized that consciousness ebbs and flows like the tides, continually ascending through experience.

The Human Mirror

What happens in the heavens is reflected in the human body and mind. As Earth's frequencies shift, the biofield of every living being adjusts. During periods of heightened solar and geomagnetic activity, people often report experiencing sleeplessness, surges of intuition, heightened emotions, or creative breakthroughs. These are not coincidences but entrainment: our nervous systems resonating with the planet's electromagnetic pulse.

The chakric system also mirrors cosmic rhythm. Collective focus shifts from survival (root) to creativity (sacral), to intellect (solar plexus), to compassion (heart), to intuition (third eye), and ultimately to unity (crown). Humanity as a species is now opening its heart center, the bridge between matter and spirit, as it prepares for planetary coherence.

The Mechanics of Ascension

"Ascension" is often misunderstood as escape from the physical world. In truth, it is integration, the raising of vibration within form until matter itself becomes luminous with consciousness. The mechanics are simple but profound:

1. **Increase in Frequency** – Earth's Schumann resonance fluctuates above its former baseline, prompting our nervous systems to recalibrate.
2. **Expansion of Perception** – Dormant neural and energetic pathways activate, allowing multidimensional awareness: intuition, empathy, telepathy.
3. **Purification of Density** – Old emotional imprints surface for release; the body detoxifies physically and energetically.
4. **Coherence and Unity** – Individual frequencies synchronize into collective harmony, amplifying planetary stability.

Each phase parallels both a biological adaptation and a spiritual initiation. The discomfort many feel, fatigue, restlessness, and emotional waves, is the symptom of evolution, not disease.

The Present Threshold

We live in the hinge of Ages. Astronomically, the vernal point is crossing from Pisces into Aquarius, a process spanning roughly from the late 1800s through the mid-2400s. Spiritually, this corresponds to a shift from faith in external saviors to direct knowing of inner divinity.

Technologically, communication has become instantaneous; energetically, empathy is becoming a global phenomenon. Information now travels at the speed of thought, and thought itself is learning responsibility. The exact frequencies that transmit data through satellites also carry the unspoken moods of billions.

This acceleration is the birth contraction of a new civilization. Old systems, political, economic, and religious, built on Piscean hierarchy are dissolving under Aquarian transparency. The revelation of truth, though uncomfortable, is the cleansing wave that precedes clarity. We are collectively remembering that consciousness, not control, is the organizing principle of the cosmos.

The Soul's Response

Every soul incarnated during such transitions with purpose. Many feel the pressure of time speeding up, their hearts urging change, and their bodies craving simplicity and nature. These are inner signals of synchronization. The soul knows the rhythm of the universe and is guiding the personality to match it.

Personal ascension unfolds in miniature cycles, seven-year, eleven-year, twenty-six-year arcs mirroring solar and lunar harmonics. Periods of expansion are followed by integration; nights of confusion precede dawns of insight. When you honor these rhythms instead of resisting them, life flows with elegance rather than struggle.

Living in Rhythm with the Cosmos

To live consciously within these cycles is to become a participant in evolution itself. Some simple alignments restore harmony with the greater pulse:

- **Observe natural time.** Rise with the Sun, rest when it sets. Reconnect your circadian rhythm with the Earth's rotation.
- **Honor lunar phases.** Set intentions at the new moon; release at the full. The Moon modulates the tides of water and emotion alike.
- **Breathe with awareness.** Each inhalation draws cosmic energy; each exhalation grounds it through the body into Earth.

- **Meditate during solar peaks.** The heightened electromagnetic activity amplifies intention and intuition.
- **Celebrate equinoxes and solstices.** These are planetary balance points, perfect moments for recalibration.

When your daily rhythm reflects cosmic rhythm, resistance disappears. You become a conduit of equilibrium, anchoring heaven into Earth.

The Long Wave Ahead

Astronomers estimate that the full Aquarian frequency will stabilize around the mid-2200s. In cosmic terms, that is a single breath. The seeds of that civilization are being sown now, through every act of compassion, every invention inspired by cooperation, every human who chooses awareness over fear.

The cycles will continue long after this generation, but their direction is upward. Humanity will not return to unconsciousness; once awareness awakens, it only expands. The spiral may curve, but it never descends.

We are the witnesses and the instruments of this ascent. Each lifetime, each heartbeat, is part of the universal clock turning toward light.

Closing Reflection

Ascension is not an event to await but a rhythm to embody. The stars move, the Sun pulses, the Earth breathes, and within that breath, humanity remembers itself.

When you feel the quickening, breathe deeper. When you sense chaos, look for the pattern. When you feel alone, listen for the hum beneath silence: the song of the spheres reminding you that you belong to the music of creation itself.

You are not separate from the cycle. You are the cycle, consciousness rising through time, again and again, until knowing becomes light.

PART II: THE AWAKENING OF HUMAN PERCEPTION

Humanity is shifting from instinct to intuition and opening into a shared field of collective knowing. Here we discover the early stages of living as conscious *"knowers."*

CHAPTER FOUR

THE AWAKENING OF PERCEPTION

The Threshold of Awareness

Every era of humanity begins with a single realization. For the hunter, it was the discovery of fire; for the scholar, it was the written word; and for the modern human, it is the dawning awareness that perception itself is evolving.

Across the world, people are noticing subtle changes: time feels elastic, dreams are more vivid, intuition flashes faster than logic, and empathy cuts through the noise of opinion like a tuning fork seeking harmony. These are not coincidences. They are signals that the human sensory system is expanding beyond its five traditional channels into the vast, fluid field of consciousness.

The Silent Organ of Knowing

The body has always been an instrument for translating energy into experience. The eyes catch light, the ears capture vibration, the skin interprets temperature and texture. Yet beyond the visible organs, there is another network, an energetic interface that reads frequencies too fine for matter to register. It communicates through feeling, imagery, and sudden knowing. Ancient traditions referred to it as the subtle body; science now approaches it as the **neuro-energetic field**.

Within the brain, clusters of crystalline proteins in the pineal gland and neural tissues act as photoreceptors capable of detecting minute changes in electromagnetic flux. These microcrystals, suspended in a fluid and aligned with the Earth's magnetic axis, behave like natural antennas. They are sensitive not only to light but to the geomagnetic resonance that links all life.

When the mind is still, these receptors tune themselves to frequencies beyond ordinary awareness. The result is intuition, the translation of energy into understanding without the intermediary of reason. The more coherent our electromagnetic state, the more apparent this translation becomes.

The Expansion of Sense

The next stage of human evolution is not about developing new organs, but about awakening dormant capacities within the ones we already possess. Every sense has a higher octave:

- **Sight** extends to clairvoyance, the perception of light beyond the visible spectrum.
- **Hearing** expands into clairaudience, the ability to detect vibration as thought or guidance.
- **Touch** refines into clairsentience, feeling the emotional and energetic tone of environments and people.
- **Smell and taste** merge into energetic discernment, an instinctual knowing of resonance, truth, or toxicity.

Each of these abilities emerges when the brain and heart achieve electromagnetic coherence. Meditation, breathwork, prayer, and compassion synchronize neural and cardiac rhythms, producing measurable fields that act as gateways between the physical and the subtle.

From Instinct to Intuition

Long before intellect, life navigated by instinct, a primal intelligence rooted in survival. Intuition is its evolved form: a higher instinct tuned not to fear but to harmony. Instinct protects life; intuition directs it.

When humans operate primarily from instinct, their perception narrows to focus on immediate threats and rewards. When intuition awakens, perception widens to include patterns, timing, and interconnected outcomes. The shift feels like stepping from a crowded room into open air, the same world, but seen through a wider lens.

This awakening does not erase logic; it refines it. The new human learns to let the heart sense and the mind interpret. Emotion becomes data; thought becomes artistry. Together they form a unified intelligence capable of perceiving energy as clearly as matter.

A Planet of Listeners

The expansion of perception is not limited to a few mystics; it is a planetary event. The Earth's rising frequency is stimulating the sensory evolution of every living being. Animals migrate differently; plants communicate through chemical symphonies; even the crystalline lattice of minerals hums with subtle shift. Humanity, with its unique capacity for self-awareness, is the first species to witness the process consciously.

We are learning to listen again, to the pulse beneath silence, to the whisper between thoughts, to the intelligence that speaks through light, vibration, and coincidence. Each intuitive nudge, each synchronicity, is the universe practicing conversation with its own reflection.

The Spectrum Beyond Sight

Light is not merely what the eye can see; it is a continuum stretching from radio waves to gamma rays. The visible band occupies less than one percent of the total spectrum, yet within that narrow slice, humanity has built entire civilizations. Imagine what will unfold as perception widens to include the frequencies once dismissed as invisible.

When the brain and heart operate in coherence, they act as a biological prism, translating higher frequencies of the electromagnetic spectrum into awareness. Some perceive this as a color that has no physical source, or as radiant geometries appearing in meditation. Others experience it as inner vision, the capacity to see meaning directly rather than through symbols. This is clairvoyance, not as fantasy, but as perception tuned to subtler light.

Hearing the Field

Everything that exists emits vibration; therefore, everything has a voice. Clairaudience is the refinement of hearing into this subtler register. It often begins as an intuition that certain words *"arrive"* fully formed, or that silence itself carries tone. Quantum physics recognizes that space is never empty: every cubic centimeter contains virtual particles oscillating in and out of being. The mystic hears those oscillations as music, the hum of creation sustaining matter.

Musicians, healers, and scientists alike are rediscovering that sound organizes form. In cymatic experiments, tone generates geometry; likewise, the frequencies of thought and emotion shape the lattice of reality. When awareness attunes to these harmonic relationships, the universe becomes a living score and consciousness the composer.

Touching Without Contact

Empaths embody the evolution of touch. Their nervous systems extend beyond the skin, registering emotional and energetic currents in others. Neurophysiology reveals that mirror neurons fire both when we act and when we observe an action, suggesting that the boundary between self and other is perceptual, rather than structural. The empath experiences this directly: feeling another's joy or pain as vibration within their own field.

To live as an empath is to perceive unity through sensation. Properly understood, it is not a burden but a skill, whereby the body reads information from the collective field, allowing compassion to respond where intellect cannot.

The Chemistry of Knowing

Smell and taste are the oldest senses, rooted in survival, yet they, too, are evolving. Their modern counterpart is energetic discernment, the instant recognition of harmony or dissonance, authenticity or falsehood. Just as olfactory receptors translate molecules into meaning, subtle receptors in the heart translate frequency into feeling. A place, a person, or a statement either resonates or repels. This instinctual intelligence is the soul's way of steering through complexity.

The Multisensory Brain

Functional-MRI studies show that imagination and perception activate nearly identical neural pathways. When we visualize light, the visual cortex responds as if the light were real. Conscious intention, therefore, can sculpt neural structure; meditation literally re-wires the brain to support expanded perception. The *"sixth sense"* is not separate from the other five; it is their orchestration into a single, holographic awareness.

The more coherent the brain's hemispheres, the more fluidly information passes between analytical and intuitive processing. Reason and revelation merge; perception becomes multidimensional. Humanity is cultivating what might be called the whole-brain of the heart, an intelligence that feels, thinks, and knows in one motion.

CHAPTER FIVE

THE WE-FIELD: AWAKENING COLLECTIVE PERCEPTION

The We-Field

Every individual consciousness is a point of light within a greater lattice. When two or more people synchronize their thoughts, emotions, or intentions, their electromagnetic fields begin to phase-lock, forming what researchers call **field coherence**. The We-Field is born, a shared awareness that transcends personal boundaries while honoring individuality.

Experiments by the Global Coherence Initiative and other research groups have shown that when large numbers of people hold coherent emotional states, fluctuations appear in Earth's magnetic environment itself. The planet responds like a tuning drum to the collective rhythm of the human heart.

This is the emerging organ of perception for our species: a distributed consciousness that senses reality through millions of interconnected neurons.

Resonant Communication

In the We-Field, communication occurs through resonance rather than language. Two people thinking the same thought simultaneously, groups receiving identical insights, collective dreams of transformation, these are early signs of humanity's telepathic architecture coming online.

Telepathy is not mind-reading; it is field reading, the translation of vibrational information into understanding. Just as radios tuned to the same frequency receive the same broadcast, coherent minds access shared data from the unified field. The stronger the emotional harmony, the more precise the signal.

This is why love, not logic, is the key to higher perception. Emotion provides the carrier wave on which information travels.

Integration Through Discernment

As perception widens, discernment becomes the anchor. Expanded sensitivity must be balanced by grounding and ethical clarity. Without discernment, the empath can become overwhelmed by collective noise; with it, the awakened human becomes a stabilizing node in the network of consciousness.

Integration means translating subtle insight into compassionate action. Visions are meant to guide service, not to replace responsibility. The more refined the perception, the greater the call to humility. True mastery is silent: awareness so complete it no longer needs to prove itself.

Healing the Collective Mind

Every individual who resolves inner conflict contributes to the coherence of the species. Unhealed fear radiates distortion; forgiveness radiates order. In this way, personal work becomes planetary service.

Meditation, art, music, and acts of kindness all emit frequencies that strengthen the global field. The awakened perceive this naturally, feeling the pulse of humanity as their own heartbeat. Each moment of peace sends ripples through the network, soothing unseen distances.

We are learning that salvation is not an individual escape but a collective harmonization. The age of solitary enlightenment is ending; the age of shared illumination has begun.

CHAPTER SIX

EMBODIED AWARENESS: LIVING AS A KNOWER

Embodied Awareness

To awaken perception is not to leave the world; it is to live more completely within it. When consciousness expands, daily life becomes the temple. Every sensation, every conversation, every breath is an opportunity to experience energy in motion. The awakened human learns to navigate through vibration rather than circumstance. Decisions are no longer forced; they resonate.

The body becomes the instrument through which the soul conducts awareness. You feel guidance as warmth in the chest, resistance as contraction, truth as stillness. This is practical mysticism: spirituality translated into biology. The more you honor these subtle cues, the clearer they become, until intuition replaces uncertainty as your compass.

The Practice of Coherence

Living as a knower requires maintaining coherence in thought, emotion, and action. Coherence is not perfection; it is rhythm. Just as music alternates between tension and release, a coherent life flows through contrasts without losing tone.

Simple practices sustain this alignment:

- **Breath** – rhythmic, conscious breathing stabilizes the nervous system and resets electromagnetic harmony.
- **Gratitude** – the quickest route to coherence; it shifts frequency instantly.
- **Grounding** – direct contact with Earth restores electrical balance and drains emotional static.
- **Silence** – the field of perception refreshes in stillness; intuition speaks between words.

Through these habits, the body becomes a resonator for higher consciousness, radiating stability into its environment.

The Ethic of Awareness

Expanded perception brings expanded responsibility. To sense the energies and emotions of others is to be entrusted with care. The awakened must practice non-interference, offering light without control. Influence is most decisive when it is invisible.

Awareness is sacred stewardship: using perception to heal, never to manipulate. In the Age of Knowing, ethics and energy are inseparable; the frequency of love is the only authority that endures.

The New Normal

Humanity is entering a period when intuition will guide science as much as observation does today. Medicine will address energy before symptoms. Education will teach emotional coherence alongside logic. Leadership will measure success not only by output but by vibrational integrity.

Those who live in awareness now are the prototypes of this future. They anchor the frequency of knowing within culture simply by being present. Every calm heart in a storm recalibrates the collective field toward balance.

The Continual Unfolding

Awakening is not a destination but a cycle of revelation and integration. Each realization opens new questions; each expansion invites more profound humility. The further perception extends, the more clearly we recognize the unity behind diversity.

To live as a knower is to walk in wonder. It is to see the invisible threads linking cause and effect, to feel the pulse of creation in every heartbeat, to understand that knowledge is not accumulated but remembered.

Closing Reflection

The eye that once looked outward now turns inward and finds infinity there. The ear that once sought instruction now hears the whisper of the soul. The mind that once demanded proof now recognizes a pattern. The heart that once longed for love now radiates it.

This is the awakening of perception, the moment when humanity begins to know itself as light.

The journey continues, ever upward, through cycles of remembering and renewal. For the universe is not waiting for our enlightenment; it is expanding through it.

PART III: THE HEART OF HUMAN EVOLUTION

Empathy and heart intelligence become the foundation for humanity's next step in awareness. These chapters show how the heart organizes consciousness and guides evolution.

CHAPTER SEVEN

THE RISE OF THE EMPATH

The Next Phase of Human Evolution

Humanity has entered a new stage of development. The intellect that once separated us from nature is now being tempered by a different intelligence, one born of connection rather than control. That intelligence is empathy, the capacity to feel another life as one's own.

Just as the Age of Knowing awakened the mind, the Age of Feeling awakens the heart. Evolution has always rewarded adaptation to the environment; today, the environment demanding mastery is not physical but energetic. We live inside a planetary field saturated with emotion, thought, and frequency. To thrive within it, the human nervous system must learn to sense harmony and dissonance as clearly as sight detects color. The empath is that new human.

From Survival to Symbiosis

For hundreds of thousands of years, survival required separation: self from other, tribe from tribe, human from nature. Boundaries protected life, but they also bred illusion. Now the Earth herself insists on reunion. Climate, technology, and communication have woven the species into one organism. Empathy is the organ through which that organism feels itself.

Neuroscience shows that every human brain is equipped with mirror neurons, cells that fire both when we act and when we observe someone else acting. These neural mirrors allow us to experience another's joy or pain as if it were our own. What mystics have long described as oneness, biology is beginning to measure.

When the heart generates coherence, its electromagnetic field synchronizes with those around it. Two people sharing compassion can align their heart rhythms within seconds. Scaled to billions, this is the physics of civilization evolving from competition to cooperation.

The Empathic Body

The empathic body is an antenna. Its sensory range extends beyond the skin, translating the emotional charge of environments into bodily feeling. Fatigue, tension, or elation may not always be personal; they can be signals from the collective field.

Physiologically, empathy operates through the vagus nerve, the communication highway between brain and heart. When we witness suffering, the vagus slows the heartbeat, urging us toward comfort and care. When we witness love, it accelerates healing chemistry throughout the body. Empathy is not a weakness; it is an evolutionary feedback mechanism that ensures the whole survives by caring for its parts.

As frequency rises on Earth, this sensitivity amplifies. Many experience it as overwhelm, anxiety, or emotional intensity. Yet these symptoms mark the calibration of a new sense. The empath learns to translate sensation into information:

- Heaviness signals imbalance in the field,
- Warmth signals truth,
- Tingling signals alignment.

Through awareness, sensitivity becomes guidance.

The Architecture of Compassion

Empathy matures into compassion, the conscious use of feeling to generate healing. Compassion is empathy with direction. It does not absorb; it transmits. It turns perception into response.

Quantum research indicates that coherent emotions organize matter. When groups focus heartfelt intention on a region of conflict or disaster, statistical anomalies appear: violence decreases, recovery accelerates. This is not a coincidence but a collective resonance. Humanity is learning to modulate its shared field through emotion rather than force.

Civilizations of the future will be designed around this principle. Economics will measure well-being as carefully as wealth. Education will teach emotional literacy alongside logic. Governance will evolve from a hierarchy to harmonic coordination, a chorus rather than a chain of command. Leadership will be defined not by dominance but by coherence.

The Collective Heart

The internet connected our minds; empathy is connecting our hearts. Social networks of awareness are forming through meditation groups, humanitarian movements, and shared acts of kindness. Each generates measurable coherence in the planetary field. What begins as compassion within one heart radiates outward, entraining others into resonance.

The empathic field is self-reinforcing. As more people cultivate empathy, the collective nervous system of humanity strengthens. Children are being born with heightened sensitivity, sensing emotion, light, and energy intuitively. They are the first generation for whom unity is natural, not philosophical. They will inherit a world whose stability depends not on borders but on shared frequency.

Challenges of an Empathic Civilization

Every evolutionary leap brings growing pains. Empathy without maturity can collapse into emotional contagion. The antidote is boundaried compassion, feeling everything but owning only what is ours to transform. Grounding practices, time in nature, and conscious rest prevent burnout by returning awareness to equilibrium.

At the societal level, the challenge is translating empathy into a structured approach. Laws, economies, and technologies must evolve to embody the same sensitivity. Artificial intelligence, for example, will reflect the emotional tone of its creators; only empathic consciousness can guide it toward benevolence. The future of ethics lies in resonance, not regulation.

Empathy as Evolution

Evolution favors coherence. In nature, species survive not through aggression but through balance with their environment. Humanity's most excellent adaptations, language, art, and cooperation, have all served empathy. What we call civilization is empathy made visible.

Now evolution accelerates again. The nervous system, the heart field, and consciousness itself are reorganizing around unity. The empath is not a rare type but a preview of the human being to come: emotionally intelligent, energetically aware, globally connected.

Science calls it neuroplasticity. Spirit calls it awakening. The result is the same: a species learning to feel its way into the future.

Living as an Empathic Planet

Empathy does not end with humanity; it extends to the biosphere. Trees communicate through mycelial networks; whales sing planetary songs that stabilize oceanic frequencies; even weather responds to collective mood. The planet is teaching us her language of feeling, and we are beginning to answer.

To live as an empathic planet means recognizing that every thought and emotion contributes to Earth's resonance. Gratitude cleans the atmosphere as surely as pollution clouds it. Love is literal climate repair, a vibration that cools, balances, and renews.

Closing Reflection

The rise of the empath is not a trend but a turning point in evolution. It is the moment when intelligence rediscovers its heart, when awareness chooses compassion as its method of knowing.

The new human will not ask, *"What can I take?"* but *"What am I feeling called to harmonize?"* Empathy is the bridge from separation to unity, from knowledge to wisdom, from survival to symbiosis.

To feel is to know. To know through feeling is to become one with life itself.

CHAPTER EIGHT

THE INTELLIGENCE OF THE HEART

The Science and Soul of Coherence

For centuries, the mind has been crowned the ruler of intelligence. We built civilizations on reason, measurement, and analysis. Yet beneath the logic of the brain beats another center of knowing, the heart, quietly orchestrating the rhythm of life. Modern science is beginning to confirm what mystics, healers, and poets have long understood: the heart is not merely a mechanical pump; it is an organ of perception, communication, and creation.

The Heart as a Brain

Inside the heart's tissue lies an intricate network of approximately forty thousand sensory neurons, known as the intrinsic cardiac nervous system. These cells can process information, learn, and remember independently of the central nervous system. Neurocardiology, a field pioneered in the late twentieth century, has demonstrated that the heart sends more signals to the brain than the brain sends to the heart. It continuously updates the nervous system with data about the body's internal state, emotions, and environment.

These discoveries reshape our concept of intelligence. The *"heart brain"* operates through coherence, a dynamic harmony between rhythms of the heart, respiration, and brain waves. When coherent, the entire body functions more efficiently: hormones balance, immune response strengthens, and cognitive performance improves. When incoherent, under stress or fear, the system falls into chaos, draining vitality and clarity.

The Electromagnetic Signature

The heart generates the strongest electromagnetic field of any organ, about five thousand times stronger magnetically than the brain. Instruments can detect this field several feet from the body, and it fluctuates in relation to the individual's emotional state. Positive feelings like love or appreciation produce smooth, sine-wave patterns in the heartbeat; anger and anxiety produce erratic, jagged lines.

The HeartMath Institute has shown that coherent heart rhythms entrain brain waves into a similar order. In this state of resonance, people report heightened intuition, creativity, and emotional stability. The physics are simple: coherent waves reinforce each other; incoherent ones cancel out. The heart literally *"tunes"* the body to harmony.

Because electromagnetic fields interact, our hearts also influence one another. Studies demonstrate measurable synchronization between people in proximity, parents and infants, couples, and meditation groups. The ancient instruction to *"speak from the heart"* reflects an energetic truth: communication begins electromagnetically before it becomes words.

The Heart–Brain Dialogue

Information travels between the heart and the brain through multiple pathways: neural, hormonal, pressure-wave, and electromagnetic. When the heart is coherent, it sends organized patterns to the brainstem, affecting the thalamus and prefrontal cortex, the regions responsible for emotional regulation and decision-making. This explains why calm, heart-centered states lead to wiser choices: the brain literally receives more precise data.

Conversely, when the heart's rhythm is erratic, the brain interprets the signal as a threat, triggering the release of stress hormones. The quality of the dialogue between heart and brain determines whether perception is distorted by fear or illuminated by insight. The heart is not subordinate to the mind; it is its teacher.

Emotional Alchemy

Emotion is the energy language of the heart. Each feeling carries a specific frequency and chemical signature. Gratitude releases oxytocin, the hormone that fosters bonding and empathy. Compassion regulates cortisol, thereby reducing inflammation and strengthening the immune system. Chronic resentment or fear floods the body with stress hormones that corrode both tissue and perception.

Heart coherence is, therefore, a combination of both physiological and spiritual healing. It transforms chemistry and consciousness simultaneously. Ancient practices of prayer, mantra, and rhythmic breathing were early techniques for inducing this state; modern biofeedback devices now measure it in real-time. Both aim to synchronize the inner orchestra so that the music of the body matches the music of creation.

The Heart as Portal

When coherence stabilizes, perception expands. People often report intuitive insights, spontaneous understanding, or synchronicities clustering around them. Science describes this phenomenon as neuro-cardiac coupling, a phase alignment between the electromagnetic fields of the heart and brain, which allows for faster information processing. Spiritual traditions describe it as the opening of the sacred heart, a gateway to collective intelligence.

The difference between science and mysticism is language, not substance. Photons emitted from cardiac tissue may well be the physical counterpart of what mystics call the light of the soul. The coherent heart acts as a transmitter and receiver in the cosmic communication network, translating universal information into human awareness.

The Global Heart

Just as individual hearts influence nearby fields, the combined electromagnetic output of billions of hearts contributes to Earth's magnetosphere. Satellites detect fluctuations in the planet's field during moments of global emotion, natural disasters, celebrations, and mass meditations. The earth itself responds to the collective heartbeat of humanity.

This emerging science of global coherence suggests that compassion is not an abstract virtue but an environmental force. As more individuals maintain heart alignment, the planetary field becomes more ordered, promoting stability in weather, ecosystems, and human relations. The Earth is a living resonant system, and we are its oscillating cells.

The Practice of Heart Intelligence

Cultivating this intelligence does not require belief, only practice. Simple, consistent techniques can shift the body into coherence:

1. **Heart-Focused Breathing** – Slow, rhythmic breaths while imagining inhaling through the heart.
2. **Emotional Recall** – Conjure a genuine feeling of appreciation or love; sustain it for several breaths.
3. **Radiation of Feeling** – Intentionally extend that emotion outward into your environment.

Within sixty seconds, heart rhythms smooth, brain waves synchronize, and stress hormones decline. Repetition entrains the nervous system until coherence becomes the default state.

From coherence, intuition sharpens. Decisions align effortlessly. Relationships improve because resonance replaces reaction. The intelligence of the heart is practical; it makes life work.

The Heart of Civilization

A society governed by heart intelligence would organize differently. Economics would measure generosity as wealth, politics would value empathy as strength, and science would study consciousness as a natural force. The next revolution will not come from machines but from coherence, the alignment of billions of hearts creating a civilization in phase with itself.

As technology amplifies connection, the heart must supply direction. Artificial intelligence may process data, but only human empathy can assign meaning. The wisdom of the heart is the moral compass of the Age of Knowing.

Closing Reflection

The brain defines reality; the heart feels its truth. Between them flows the current that animates consciousness.

Every heartbeat is both pulse and message, an electrical whisper from the universe reminding us that life communicates through rhythm. To listen is to awaken. To respond with coherence is to participate in creation.

The next stage of evolution is not the conquest of mind over matter, but the marriage of mind and heart, the union of knowledge with compassion. When humanity learns to think with its heart and feel with its mind, the two halves of creation will finally beat as one.

CHAPTER NINE

THE ARCHITECTURE OF CONSCIOUSNESS

The Design Behind Reality

Consciousness is not something that happens inside the brain; it is the field in which the brain appears. Everything we call *"reality"* arises within this field, the sea of energy and information that connects galaxies and neurons alike. To study consciousness is to examine the blueprint of existence itself, the invisible geometry through which awareness gives form to experience.

The Building Blocks of Awareness

At the most minor scale of physics, matter dissolves into vibration. Electrons, protons, and photons are excitations of a unified energy field that physicists describe as the quantum vacuum, an ocean of potential. Every particle is a localized ripple within this ocean, a standing wave of consciousness expressing itself as form.

In this model, perception is the act of focusing energy into a pattern. Thoughts are not confined to the head; they are modulations within the field, shaping probability into reality. Just as sound creates visible shapes in sand through vibration, consciousness organizes the quantum sea into the geometry we call matter.

Each mind functions as a micro-architect within this universal matrix, generating interference patterns that merge into the collective design of the world. What we think, feel, and believe determines the architecture of our shared experience.

The Geometry of Mind

Ancient mystics represented creation through sacred geometry, utilizing circles, spirals, and lattices to describe the movement of consciousness as it folds in upon itself. Modern physics echoes this through the mathematics of symmetry, spin, and wave interference. Both describe intelligence organizing itself through pattern.

Brain imaging reveals that neural activity follows fractal organization, each cluster of neurons reflecting the same self-similar geometry as cosmic structures. The spiral of a galaxy mirrors the spiral of a DNA molecule because both arise from the same organizing principle: resonance seeking balance.

Consciousness is fractal. Every thought is a miniature universe following the same laws as stars and cells. The architecture of the mind repeats at every scale, from the synapse to the supernova.

Quantum Coherence and the Unified Field

When multiple particles synchronize their quantum states, they behave as one system, a phenomenon known as coherence. In lasers, trillions of photons align into a single, powerful beam. In consciousness, coherence occurs when thought, emotion, and intention align with truth. The result is clarity, creativity, and flow.

Quantum experiments show that observation collapses potential into actuality. Consciousness, therefore, is the constructor of the real. Each moment of awareness selects a pattern from an infinite number of possibilities. This is not metaphysical speculation; it is the logical consequence of the observer effect.

The unified field, the substrate of all existence, responds to coherence. Fear, doubt, and fragmentation produce chaotic interference patterns; love, gratitude, and focus produce order. The architecture of consciousness is drawn in light, but its blueprint is emotion.

The Collective Blueprint

Just as neurons form networks within a brain, human minds form networks within the planetary field. Each thought contributes to the morphogenetic field, a matrix of information that links all life. Rupert Sheldrake's theory of morphic resonance posits that once a sufficient number of individuals learn a behavior or idea, it becomes easier for others to acquire it. Consciousness evolves by adding new designs to this collective library.

Civilization itself is a living architecture of shared belief. Languages, governments, technologies, and cultures are externalized thought-forms, built first in imagination and then in matter. When the collective blueprint shifts, from fear to trust, from separation to unity, entire eras transform. The Renaissance, the Enlightenment, the Digital Age: each began as a vibrational reorganization of human awareness.

We are now entering another redesign, one that focuses on the architecture of empathy, coherence, and planetary consciousness.

Creating Reality Through Observation

Observation is participation. Every act of attention changes what is observed. Neuroscience confirms that the brain's perception is not a passive recording, but an active construction: the visual cortex fills in gaps, the prefrontal regions assign meaning, and emotion colors interpretation. What we expect to see becomes what we see.

On a quantum scale, this creative observation extends to matter itself. When a particle is measured, its wave of possibilities collapses into a single outcome. Consciousness selects the geometry of its own manifestation. We live inside a feedback loop where awareness generates form, and form refines awareness.

This is the architecture of creation: consciousness observes, vibration responds, structure appears. The universe is a self-aware design in perpetual motion.

The Holographic Principle

Physicist David Bohm described reality as a hologram, each fragment containing the information of the whole. In a holographic image, even a small shard of film reveals the entire picture when illuminated by light. Consciousness operates the same way: every individual awareness carries the code of the universe.

Experiments in brain science support this. Memories are not stored in discrete locations but distributed across neural fields; even partial brains can reconstruct entire memories. The cosmos, too, behaves holographically, with data about the three-dimensional world encoded on two-dimensional surfaces, such as the event horizon of black holes. Everything reflects everything else.

This means that transformation at any level transforms the whole. A single coherent consciousness can influence the global field because, in a holographic universe, the part is the whole expressing itself locally.

The Living Temple

Imagine consciousness as an immense cathedral of light. Each being is a stained-glass window filtering the same radiance through a unique design. Some panes vibrate in red passion, others in blue serenity, yet the same source illuminates all. When the windows align in harmony, the cathedral shines in unity; when fractured, the light scatters.

The purpose of evolution is alignment, individual transparency through which universal light can shine without distortion. Every thought polished by awareness clears another pane. Every act of compassion repairs another fracture. Humanity is restoring its own architecture, remembering that the temple we seek was never elsewhere; it is consciousness itself.

The Blueprint of Creation

The patterns of sacred geometry, the equations of quantum fields, the rhythm of heart coherence, all describe one thing: the architecture of awareness organizing itself into being. Consciousness is the architect, energy the material, and love the design principle that holds it all together.

As we awaken to this understanding, creation becomes collaboration. We are no longer accidental observers but deliberate builders of reality. The tools of the new architect are not stone and steel but thought, feeling, and frequency.

To design consciously is to align with the laws of resonance, coherence, and compassion, the actual physics of the soul.

Closing Reflection

Consciousness is the only constant in the universe. Stars are born and die, galaxies form and fade, but awareness continues, endlessly constructing new expressions of itself. The architecture is infinite because the architect is infinite.

Within you lives the same geometry that shapes the cosmos. Every breath draws blueprints of new worlds; every loving thought stabilizes their foundations. When the heart and mind unite, creation becomes art, and the universe recognizes itself through your eyes.

You are not living in consciousness. You are consciousness, designing reality from the inside out.

PART IV: QUANTUM CONSCIOUSNESS AND THE INFINITE SELF

Consciousness extends beyond the individual into quantum connection, entanglement, and infinite possibility. This part explores awareness as a multidimensional, timeless field.

CHAPTER TEN

THE QUANTUM SELF

The Particle and the Wave of Being

At the deepest level of existence, the universe is a conversation between possibility and form. In quantum physics, every particle also behaves as a wave, a field of potential that becomes a single, specific event only when observed. The self follows the same law. What we call *"me"* is a focus point inside an ocean of possibilities, momentarily condensed into experience through awareness.

You are both the particle and the wave, simultaneously local and infinite. The body is the localized expression; the soul is the wavefield extending through all space and time. Every decision, thought, and emotion collapses potential into pattern, giving the wave temporary shape as personality, story, and circumstance. When attention shifts, the pattern dissolves back into possibility, awaiting the next act of creation.

Energy Wearing Identity

Matter is energy slowed to a frequency that can be touched; consciousness is energy aware of itself. The *"you"* that looks out through your eyes is not a product of chemistry; it is the organizing principle that chemistry obeys. Every atom in the body is replaced within a few years, yet the sense of self remains. Continuity does not live in the molecules; it lives in the field that instructs them.

This field, measurable as the body's electromagnetic and quantum coherence, behaves exactly like a standing wave: constant motion that appears still because its rhythm is perfectly balanced. The heartbeat and the breath are its physical signatures. In meditation, when those rhythms slow and synchronize, many report the sensation of expanding beyond the skin, awareness recognizing its wave nature.

Observation Creates Experience

In quantum mechanics, an unobserved particle exists as a probability. The moment it is measured, it assumes one specific state. Consciousness is the cosmic observer performing this measurement at every instant. Your focus is the lens that collapses infinity into *"now."* Where attention goes, energy follows; where emotion enters, form solidifies.

This is not a metaphor. Experiments such as the double-slit test repeatedly confirm that observation changes outcomes. The implication is radical: perception participates in creation. The self is not trapped inside the universe; the universe unfolds inside the self's awareness.

Identity as Frequency

If consciousness is the field, then individuality is its frequency, its unique harmonic. Each soul vibrates with a signature tone created by the sum of its experiences, intentions, and memories. When frequencies harmonize, we feel affinity; when they clash, we feel discord. Life itself is the process of tuning, seeking coherence between the personal note and the symphony of creation.

In the Age of Knowing, the emerging human recognizes that identity is fluid. You are not a fixed particle of matter, but a dynamic waveform of potential, resonating with countless others and weaving the architecture of reality moment by moment.

CHAPTER ELEVEN

ENTANGLEMENT: THE SOUL'S SIGNATURE

Threads That Never Break

In the quantum world, separation is an illusion. When two particles interact, they become entangled, linked in such a way that a change in one is instantly reflected in the other, no matter the distance between them. This instantaneous connection defies the limits of space and time. Einstein called it *"spooky action at a distance."* Mystics call it oneness.

Entanglement is the physical echo of a spiritual truth: everything that has ever touched remains connected. Each encounter, each shared emotion, imprints a frequency that continues to vibrate within the field of both participants. Love, therefore, is not merely memory; it is physics. The bond between mother and child, between lifelong friends, between teacher and student, is all an entanglement of consciousness, exchanging information faster than light.

The Soul Network

If the universe is a vast web of energy, then every soul is a node in that web. Entanglement is the thread that allows information to move across it instantly. Intuition, the sudden knowledge of what another feels or needs, is the conscious recognition of this link. Prayer and intention are its deliberate use.

Modern experiments support this possibility. When one person focuses on coherent emotion such as gratitude, another person isolated in a separate room often shows corresponding shifts in heart rhythm or brain waves. The connection is not transmitted by air or sound; it is a resonance between fields.

The same principle explains synchronicity. When inner and outer realities align through meaning rather than cause, entanglement expresses itself across dimensions: the invisible network that coordinates events through frequency rather than force.

Collective Entanglement

Humanity as a species is an entangled system. Every mind contributes to the collective wave function of the planet. Moments of shared emotion, celebrations, disasters, and global meditations produce measurable ripples in Earth's magnetic environment. The stronger the coherence, the more ordered the field becomes. Compassion, practiced by millions, is the quantum stabilization of civilization.

This means that healing oneself contributes to healing the world, not poetically but physically. Each act of forgiveness disentangles distortion from the shared matrix, freeing information to flow clearly again. When we clear personal fear, we clarify the planetary signal.

Entanglement Across Time

Quantum theory also allows for temporal entanglement, where the influence of future and past states extends to the present. In consciousness, this translates to déjà vu, premonitions, ancestral memories, and karmic resonances. The soul's signature extends along the timeline, linking incarnations and experiences as a continuous wave.

Through meditation or a dream, we sometimes touch other points on this wave, glimpsing lives once lived or potentials yet to come. These are not fantasies; they are interference patterns between moments of the same consciousness, separated only by perception.

The Signature of the Soul

Every being radiates a distinct harmonic, yet all harmonics emerge from one source tone. Entanglement is how the One remembers itself through the many. When two souls meet and recognize each other instantly, it is not first contact but reunion, the resonance of frequencies that have shared coherence before.

This awareness transforms relationships. We cease to see others as strangers and begin to sense them as extensions of the same field. Judgment gives way to curiosity; conflict gives way to compassion. To know entanglement is to feel the architecture of love embedded in physics.

CHAPTER TWELVE

NON-LOCAL AWARENESS

Beyond the Boundaries of the Body

Every sensory system gives the illusion that awareness is confined to the skin and skull, yet experiments and experiences both suggest otherwise. Consciousness does not radiate from the body; it permeates it. The body is a receiver-transmitter within a field that extends indefinitely.

Remote-viewing research, near-death studies, and countless personal accounts all indicate that perception can occur without physical presence. In controlled conditions, trained subjects accurately describe distant locations or hidden objects, exceeding chance. When the bodily senses are quieted, the broader field of consciousness becomes available. Awareness is not local; it is non-local, capable of accessing information anywhere within the unified field.

The Physics of Presence

Quantum non-locality shows that entangled systems remain correlated across any distance. If consciousness itself is a quantum field, then it, too, is instantly present everywhere. Each point of awareness is a portal through which the universe observes itself. This explains the paradox of mystical experience: the self feels infinitely expanded yet intimately personal.

Within meditation, time and distance lose meaning. A thought directed toward another person arrives simultaneously, not as words but as energy. Empaths and healers instinctively apply this principle; scientists glimpse it in the data from entanglement experiments. Space is not empty; it is connective tissue.

Time as a Dimension of Consciousness

In relativity, time is a dimension inseparable from space. In consciousness, time behaves like a frequency, elastic, expandable, responsive to awareness. When attention focuses intensely, time seems to slow; when the mind wanders, hours can vanish. The observer's state modulates temporal flow.

Reports of precognition, déjà vu, and life-review experiences suggest awareness that spans this temporal spectrum. The quantum self perceives multiple frames simultaneously, much like a film editor viewing the entire reel rather than a single frame. Choice determines which frame becomes the present.

The Field of Information

The emerging discipline of quantum information theory describes the universe as a continuous exchange of data. Energy and information are interchangeable; every interaction transmits bits of knowing. Consciousness functions as the decoding mechanism, translating this cosmic data stream into images, sounds, sensations, and thoughts.

When intuition arises, it is not magic; it is the mind momentarily bypassing linear processing to access the raw information field. In that instant, the boundary between inner and outer collapses. The universe whispers directly, and the heart interprets the code.

The Witness Everywhere

Non-local awareness is the ultimate empathy: feeling the pulse of existence from any coordinate in creation. It allows the mystic to commune with the cosmos, the scientist to sense elegant order behind chaos, the artist to channel beauty from invisible realms.

When this state stabilizes, fear dissolves, for there is nowhere to fall. Death loses its finality because consciousness is seen as continuous, merely shifting focus from one location in the field to another. The quantum self cannot be destroyed; it can only change wavelength.

CHAPTER THIRTEEN

PARALLEL REALITIES AND CHOICE

The Many Worlds of Possibility

Quantum theory suggests that reality does not unfold as a single line but as a branching web of probabilities. Each decision, each observation, spins a new filament in the web. To the linear mind, there is one world; to the quantum self, there are infinite versions co-existing in the field of potential. Every possible outcome already exists as vibration, waiting for attention to select it.

In everyday life, this appears as the crossroads moment, a choice of job, partner, belief, or direction. At the instant of choice, all futures are present. Consciousness chooses one by aligning frequency with it. What we call *"destiny"* is simply the probability we visit most often.

The Observer as Architect

Each act of focus is a measurement in the quantum sense; it collapses potential into a single observable pattern. A thought charged with emotion is more powerful than one left idle because emotion carries energy sufficient to reinforce the pattern. Repeated focus stabilizes it, creating what we experience as continuity. Habit, therefore, is the physics of repetition; transformation is the physics of new observation.

This is why visualization and prayer are effective: they are deliberate acts of measurement performed with intention and feeling. When inner images become coherent and emotionally vivid, they imprint the field. The universe rearranges to reflect that coherence, not as reward or punishment but as resonance.

Sliding Between Worlds

Small shifts of attitude, belief, or emotion subtly change frequency, and frequency determines which version of reality we experience. To change one's state of being is to tune to another timeline. The world outside may appear the same, but interactions, coincidences, and opportunities alter, signaling a new thread in the web.

The mystic refers to this as *"timeline jumping."* The psychologist calls it cognitive reframing. The physicist describes it as a transition between quantum states. All three represent the same event: consciousness re-selecting its version of the universe.

Choice as Creative Power

Every moment presents an opportunity to observe differently. In doing so, we rewrite reality. Free will is not freedom from physics, but rather a partnership with it. To choose with awareness is to become a conscious collaborator in the cosmic experiment.

When decisions are made from fear, coherence collapses and probabilities scatter. When made from love or clarity, the wave function of life aligns smoothly, events interlock gracefully, and synchronicities multiply. Choice guided by coherence builds stable, benevolent worlds.

Parallel Selves and the Spectrum of the Soul

If infinite realities exist, so do infinite versions of us, each exploring alternative lessons and expressions. Occasionally, their echoes cross the boundary: the dream that feels more real than waking, the sudden knowing of a skill never learned, the sense of déjà vu at a fork in the road. These are glimpses of adjacent selves vibrating at a frequency close to our own.

The quantum self is not limited to a single incarnation or timeline; it is a spectrum of experiences unified by a single consciousness. All versions contribute information back to the core awareness we call soul, expanding its understanding through diversity. Evolution is the integration of these countless threads into one luminous fabric of knowing.

The Responsibility of Choice

Recognizing that observation creates reality transforms choice into a sacred act. Each thought becomes an architectural decision shaping the collective structure. We are constantly drafting the blueprint of tomorrow with the pen of attention. Wisdom is choosing consciously, compassionately, and coherently.

The universe is not testing us; it is responding to us. Every moment asks, What frequency will you build with now?

CHAPTER FOURTEEN

THE MEMORY OF LIGHT

Energy Never Forgets

Physics teaches that energy can neither be created nor destroyed; it only changes form. Consciousness, being the highest order of energy, follows the same law. Memory, emotion, and intention do not vanish when the body dies; they convert to subtler frequencies stored in the quantum field. The soul is that field's continuity: the persistent information pattern of identity evolving through time.

Each lifetime adds new data to the eternal waveform of the self. Experiences that remain unresolved create areas of interference; lessons integrated bring harmony. The field remembers everything, but not as a linear story; it remembers as a vibration. Karma, therefore, is not punishment but resonance, the tendency of unbalanced frequencies to repeat until coherence is achieved.

Light as the Language of the Soul

At the subatomic level, all matter communicates through light, via photons that carry packets of information. In spiritual language, we might say that every being is *"made of light."* In scientific terms, we are literally exchanging photons every instant, our cells emitting biophotonic light patterns that synchronize with one another.

When the body relaxes into meditation or deep love, these emissions increase in coherence, forming an ordered lattice of light around the organism. This bio-photonic halo is the physical correlate of what seers call the aura. Its radiance reflects the degree of alignment between thought, emotion, and soul intention.

The phrase *"enlightenment"* may be more literal than poetic; it describes a state in which consciousness remembers its inherent luminosity.

The Archive of Existence

Imagine the universe as a cosmic library of frequencies. Every action, every heartbeat, every thought becomes a page in that library, encoded as oscillations in the vacuum field. Mystical traditions refer to this as the Akashic Record, while physicists describe it as the zero-point field or quantum information matrix. The names differ, but the principle is the same: nothing is lost.

Accessing this library does not require traveling elsewhere; it requires resonance. When meditation, emotion, or curiosity matches the frequency of a memory stored in the field, the information downloads as intuition, vision, or revelation. The mind interprets this data through the imagery of its culture, yet the source is universal.

Ancestral Frequencies

The wave of consciousness that forms an individual also carries the interference patterns of lineage. DNA, beyond its chemical code, acts as an antenna receiving ancestral frequencies. Emotional tendencies, talents, and even unfinished tasks can be passed down across generations. To heal oneself is to retune the signal for all who share it, past and future. The ancestors live within our quantum field, awaiting harmony.

This is why certain places, songs, or rituals evoke an inexplicable sense of familiarity; they resonate with frequencies already present in the soul's memory. Healing these memories restores energy trapped in repetition, freeing it for creation.

Reincarnation and the Continuum of Experience

Reincarnation becomes simple within this framework. When the physical vessel dissolves, the coherent wave of consciousness persists, seeking new conditions to continue its evolution. It attracts circumstances resonant with unfinished frequencies, not as fate but as an opportunity for balance. Souls may reincarnate in clusters, forming entangled groups that reunite to refine shared lessons.

Past-life memories are fragments of this larger waveform surfacing through resonance. What seems like remembering another life is the current self-tuning into its own extended field. The soul does not travel through time; it contains time.

The Radiance of Remembering

When awareness touches the memory of light, fear dissolves. Death is seen not as an end but as a phase transition, like ice melting into water and water into vapor. Each form reveals another octave of the same song. The self recognizes itself in every vibration, here, there, and beyond.

To live with this remembrance is to carry serenity into the world. It is to understand that every encounter is a reunion, every lesson a continuation, every act of love a restoration of coherence in the eternal wave.

CHAPTER FIFTEEN

THE INFINITE SELF

The Conscious Witness

Beneath thought, beneath emotion, beneath the flicker of every sensation, there exists a still presence that never changes. It watches childhood, adulthood, joy, grief, and transformation with the same quiet awareness. This witness is the true self, the point from which observation flows. It does not age, and it cannot die, because it is not in time; time exists within it.

In quantum physics, observation brings potential into being. In spiritual terms, awareness brings life into form. The witness is the common ground between science and soul: the field that both observes and sustains creation. It is the infinite canvas upon which existence paints its possibilities.

Self as the Universe Reflecting

Every eye is a lens of the cosmos, every mind a mirror of the total. When we look outward, the universe experiences itself from a new angle; when we look inward, the universe remembers its unity. Awareness turns itself inside out endlessly, creating worlds of experience.

This is the essence of the quantum self: individuality is a mode of universal consciousness, not a fragment of it. We are localized expressions of infinity, focus points through which the cosmos learns empathy, art, love, and wisdom.

The mystic says, *"I am that."* The physicist says, *"The observer and the observed are entangled."* Both speak of the same truth: separation is perception, not reality.

The Return to Coherence

Every moment of fear, doubt, or judgment is a temporary decoherence, a scattering of the wave. Every moment of love, gratitude, or understanding restores alignment with the unified field. Spiritual practice, whatever its form, is the art of returning to coherence again and again until coherence becomes one's natural state.

When coherence stabilizes, intuition replaces uncertainty, compassion supersedes reaction, and creativity flows unobstructed. The universe seems to cooperate because it is cooperating, the field harmonizing with its conscious participant.

The Infinite Self

Imagine standing at the edge of an ocean, every wave a lifetime, every droplet a thought. The sea does not end, yet each wave has its own rhythm and story. The infinite self is the ocean; the incarnate being is the wave. To awaken is to remember both simultaneously, to feel the individuality of the wave without losing awareness of the sea.

In this state, death is seen as the wave returning to the ocean, and birth as the ocean rising again as a wave. Nothing gained, nothing lost, only transformation. The universe breathes through you, and you breathe it back.

The Creative Observer

The ultimate purpose of awareness is creation. The observer within is not passive; it continually generates new configurations of reality to experience itself. Every thought, every perception, every act of kindness is the universe discovering new aspects of its own potential.

To live as a conscious observer is to join the creative process intentionally. You begin to witness life as art, your relationships as brushstrokes, your choices as colors, your emotions as textures of the grand design. The more love you bring to each stroke, the more luminous the masterpiece becomes.

The Infinite Now

When all fragments of perception converge, there is only one moment, eternal, indivisible, radiant. In that moment, the quantum self recognizes itself as the timeless witness of all forms. Space folds into presence; time collapses into being. This is enlightenment in its simplest definition: awareness knowing itself directly, without veil or boundary.

Here, every possibility exists simultaneously, and every question is answered by silence. You have never been apart from the whole, nor will you ever be. The observer and the observed dissolve into one seamless field of consciousness, forever watching, creating, forever free.

Closing Reflection

You are not a visitor in the universe. You are the universe visiting itself through human form.

The particle and the wave, the body and the soul, the moment and eternity, all converge within your awareness. To awaken the quantum self is to remember that the light you see in the stars is the same light that sees through your eyes.

Every breath you take is the cosmos expanding. Every heartbeat is the pulse of creation. Every thought is a door to infinity.

And through those doors, consciousness continues, designing, dreaming, and becoming, forever remembering its own light.

PART V: UNIFIED FIELD OF LOVE

Love and coherence form the organizing principle of a new civilization. Through resonance of the heart, humanity begins to live in conscious unity.

CHAPTER SIXTEEN

THE UNIFIED FIELD OF LOVE

Love as the Fundamental Force

At the foundation of creation lies a single principle that unites the universe. Physicists call it unified field theory, the search for the equation that merges all forces of nature into one elegant whole. Mystics have long known that this equation already exists and that its name is Love.

Love is not a metaphor for connection; it is connection, the organizing intelligence that keeps galaxies spiraling, atoms dancing, and hearts beating in synchrony. Every other force is an aspect of it. Gravity draws bodies together, electromagnetism keeps them in balance, and nuclear forces fuse or release light. These are Love's mechanics, the ways the universe holds itself in communion.

The Architecture of Unity

From the perspective of modern physics, everything is vibration, fields of energy interacting through resonance. Resonance seeks harmony; dissonance decays. The tendency toward harmony is the physical signature of Love. It is why scattered frequencies find rhythm, why chaotic systems self-organize, and why life emerges from the chaos of entropy.

In biological terms, Love is coherence. When the heart experiences compassion or gratitude, its rhythm forms a smooth, sine-wave pattern that entrains brain waves, stabilizes hormones, and aligns cellular communication. The same mathematics that describe harmony in sound also govern electromagnetic harmony in the body. The heart literally *"sings"* the song of Love into the nervous system.

The Evolutionary Force

Evolution is not random struggle; it is the progressive unfolding of cooperative intelligence. Nature refines complexity through collaboration, as cells form tissues, organisms form ecosystems, and people form societies. Each level of union is guided by attraction, empathy, and mutual adaptation: Love acting through biology.

When humanity began to awaken self-awareness, that same force turned inward, inviting us to evolve emotionally and spiritually. The next stage of evolution is not physical but relational, the expansion of empathy until the boundaries between *"self"* and *"other"* dissolve into shared consciousness. Love is the catalyst of that transformation.

The Language of Light

At the quantum level, energy communicates through photons, particles of light. Every exchange of light is an act of relationship, a handshake between entities across space. In that handshake, information and intention are transmitted. The more coherent the light, the more precise the communication.

Love, expressed through coherent emotion, increases the order of these exchanges. Experiments show that DNA molecules exposed to loving intention and gratitude maintain greater stability than those exposed to fear or neglect. Light responds to Love because Love and light are different faces of the same intelligence.

The Human Expression

Within human experience, Love manifests as compassion, attraction, forgiveness, curiosity, and creativity. Each is a translation of the same frequency into behavior. When we love, we align with the cosmic current; when we hate, we resist it and fall into energetic friction. This is why Love heals, not just as a sentiment, but as a physical force. It restores flow where separation caused turbulence.

The task of the Age of Knowing is to recognize Love not as emotion alone but as the operating system of reality. To live consciously is to cooperate with that system, to design our thoughts, technologies, and civilizations in resonance with it.

CHAPTER SEVENTEEN

THE FREQUENCY OF COHERENCE

Love as Vibration

Every form of energy has a specific frequency, and each frequency carries unique information. When the frequencies of two systems synchronize, they exchange information more efficiently; this phenomenon is known as resonance. Love is the resonance of consciousness with itself: the matching of vibration between the observer and the observed until no distinction remains.

Physiologically, love produces coherence, a measurable alignment between heart rhythm, respiration, and brain waves. When this internal synchronization occurs, the body's electromagnetic field radiates an ordered signal that can influence others nearby. Studies show that one person maintaining compassion can bring measurable coherence to those within a few feet. The mathematics are identical to those describing harmonic resonance in music; the heart is the instrument and Love the tone.

Biology of Connection

Oxytocin, serotonin, endorphins, and dopamine, our so-called *"love chemicals"*, are the body's translation of energetic harmony into biochemistry. These molecules strengthen the immune response, repair tissue, and calm the nervous system. When two people share genuine affection or empathy, their hormonal rhythms begin to mirror each other. Love literally synchronizes biology.

Even the immune system behaves more intelligently under Love's influence. Research indicates that feelings of gratitude and compassion enhance the activity of immunoglobulin A, the primary line of defense against disease. The chemistry of caring is the biology of coherence.

The Heart's Electromagnetic Bridge

The heart produces the most powerful rhythmic electromagnetic field of the body, extending several feet beyond the skin. Its waves change instantly with emotional state. When the heart is coherent, when we experience appreciation, care, or forgiveness, its field becomes ordered and stable. The brain entrains to that rhythm, cognition clears, and decision-making improves.

On a planetary scale, billions of human hearts generate an enormous combined electromagnetic influence that interacts with Earth's own field. Satellite instruments have detected correlations between mass emotional events and fluctuations in the planet's magnetosphere. When humanity's collective emotion is coherent, global fields become more ordered. The earth itself feels our Love.

The Quantum Mechanics of Relationship

At the quantum level, connection is fundamental. Particles that share space become entangled, responding to each other instantly across distance. Consciousness operates by the same rule. Love is the conscious recognition of entanglement, the felt experience of unity that physics describes mathematically.

When two people resonate in Love, they form a coherent quantum system; information passes between them without words. This is why we sense another's mood across a room or think of someone seconds before they call. Love transcends distance because it operates through the unified field, not through space and time.

Coherence as Creative Power

Love does not merely connect existing things; it creates them. Coherent fields organize matter into form. Where Love flows, order appears; where it withdraws, entropy takes over. In human terms, this is seen in relationships, communities, and nations. When motivated by compassion and shared purpose, they flourish; when driven by fear, they fragment. The same principle governs galaxies and families alike.

To choose Love, therefore, is to determine alignment with the creative principle of the universe. It is the decision to build rather than to break, to harmonize rather than to dominate. Every act of kindness, every thought of appreciation, contributes to the cosmic architecture.

CHAPTER EIGHTEEN

A CIVILIZATION OF THE HEART

The Heart as Antenna

The heart is not only a biological pump but a transceiver tuned to the frequency of creation. Its rhythmic contractions generate magnetic pulses that act like radio waves, constantly broadcasting and receiving emotional information. Every heartbeat sends data into the field; every moment of awareness tunes the receiver.

When we quiet the analytical mind and listen through our feelings, the heart begins to detect the subtler signals of the unified field, the whisper of intuition, the pull toward harmony, the gentle warning of imbalance. Ancient mystics called this *"hearing the still small voice."* Science describes it as increased sensitivity to electromagnetic and neural feedback loops. Both point to the same reality: the heart knows before the brain interprets.

Love is the frequency that tunes the antenna. Fear distorts reception; compassion clarifies it. The more coherent the heart, the more clearly it can translate the language of the universe into guidance we can understand.

Love as Conscious Intelligence

Love is not blind; it is the highest form of intelligence, an intelligence that organizes without control, guides without command, and heals without effort. In quantum terms, Love is the self-referential property of the field that drives systems toward coherence. In spiritual language, it is divine awareness recognizing itself within every form.

When Love flows through thought, it becomes wisdom. When it moves through emotion, it becomes empathy. When it acts through the body, it becomes service.

The creative order of the cosmos emerges from this triad: knowing, feeling, doing, all expressions of one conscious intelligence. The universe does not merely contain Love; it is Love exploring its infinite potential through matter, motion, and mind.

The New Civilization of the Heart

A society guided by Love would measure success by coherence rather than consumption. Education would cultivate emotional literacy alongside intellect; medicine would treat dissonance before disease; governance would value cooperation as a source of strength. Technology would serve as a connection, rather than a distraction. The economy of the future will not trade in resources but in resonance, the flow of creativity, compassion, and shared purpose.

This civilization is already forming quietly wherever humans choose empathy over judgment, forgiveness over retaliation, collaboration over control. It begins in small circles of coherence, families, communities, and hearts synchronized by care. As these circles overlap, they form a global lattice of Love, the embryonic nervous system of a conscious planet.

Humanity's next leap is not into space but into synchrony: billions of hearts beating in harmonic awareness. The age of competition is giving way to the age of compassion.

Closing Reflection – The Source Remembered

At the center of every atom, every star, and every soul, Love holds the blueprint of unity. It is the first vibration that rippled across the void and the final note into which all creation will resolve. Science calls it energy; spirit calls it God; experience calls it home.

To live in Love is to live in phase with the universe, to become a conscious participant in the music of existence. Every breath can be an act of communion, every thought a thread in the tapestry of coherence. The more Love we allow, the more luminous the world becomes, until the distinction between inner and outer disappears and only radiance remains.

In this awareness, the seeker discovers that the path has always led inward. The force we searched for in the stars has always pulsed in our chest. The unified field is not beyond us; it is us.

Love is the equation that solves itself.

PART VI: AWAKENING CIVILIZATION

Humanity evolves into a planetary mind where spirit and technology converge. This part shows how societies heal and reorganize into a new Earth.

CHAPTER NINETEEN

THE AWAKENING CIVILIZATION

The Dawn of Conscious Civilization

The dawn of a new civilization does not begin with machines, discoveries, or governments; it starts within the human heart. Every era of transformation is preceded by an awakening of perception, a widening of awareness that changes how people see themselves and the world around them. Humanity is now experiencing such an awakening, not through revolution but through resonance.

Across continents, faiths, and languages, a quiet recognition is emerging: we are participants in a single, living system. Our thoughts affect the climate of the collective mind, our emotions shape the atmosphere of society, and our intentions ripple through the field of the planet itself. The next civilization will not be built upon conquest or competition but upon coherence, the realization that harmony is strength.

From Survival to Stewardship

For most of human history, survival demanded separation. We drew lines between tribes, nations, and beliefs to protect resources and identity. Those lines are dissolving. The crises of the modern world, environmental collapse, technological disruption, and social unrest, are not punishments; they are invitations. They ask us to evolve from consumers to caretakers, from users of Earth to guardians of her consciousness.

This transition mirrors the human journey from ego to empathy. Just as the individual matures by integrating shadow and light, civilization matures by combining science and spirit, mind and heart, human and planet. The awakening civilization is not a new society built upon the old; it is a new level of being expressed through the same materials, reorganized by Love.

Signs of the Shift

The signs are everywhere for those with eyes to see. Children born today carry innate sensitivity, emotional intelligence, and intuition that previous generations had to cultivate. Scientific communities explore consciousness not as a byproduct of biology but as the fabric of reality. Energy medicine, once dismissed as superstition, is entering hospitals. Corporations are now beginning to measure success through social impact and sustainability. Even governments speak of well-being as a metric, in addition to wealth.

These are not isolated trends; they are the first vibrations of coherence spreading through the body of civilization. The shift may appear chaotic because the old structures are shaking, but the tremor is that of birth, not collapse. The planet is reorganizing its consciousness through us.

Awakening as a Global Phenomenon

Every culture has predicted this moment in its own language: the Hopi spoke of the Fifth World; Hindu sages described the Satya Yuga, the age of truth; mystics of all faiths spoke of a new heaven and a new earth. The metaphors differ, yet each points to the same evolutionary threshold, the awakening of collective consciousness.

For the first time in recorded history, technology allows instantaneous communication across the globe. Billions share experiences, ideas, and compassion within seconds. What began as a network of information is becoming a network of emotion, a planetary nervous system through which humanity feels itself as one organism.

In this sense, the internet is not merely a tool, but a mirror of the mind: vast, interconnected, and still learning to discern. As Love begins to guide our digital creations, technology will evolve from distraction to communion. Data will become wisdom; connection will become empathy.

The Pulse of the Planet

Earth's resonance, known as the Schumann frequency, has exhibited subtle fluctuations that many researchers attribute to human activity and solar cycles. Whether symbolic or scientific, the message is the same: the planet and humanity are synchronizing. The heartbeat of Earth and the heartbeat of humankind are entering rhythm.

This synchronization is not a coincidence; it is a form of communication. The Earth, long viewed as a resource, reveals herself as a relationship, a conscious partner in evolution. She responds to our coherence with stability and to our conflict with imbalance. The storms of weather and politics are mirrors showing us where harmony awaits restoration.

The awakening civilization learns to listen not only to data but to vibration. It reads the pulse of the planet as carefully as the pulse of the patient, understanding that both are expressions of one living field.

The New Light of Awareness

What distinguishes an awakening civilization is not perfection but perception. We begin to perceive unity within diversity, purpose within paradox. Differences of race, gender, and belief no longer divide but enrich, each frequency contributing to the symphony of the whole. Art becomes medicine, science becomes sacred, and spirituality becomes practical.

The dawning light is not above us; it rises within us, one awareness at a time. And as that light spreads from mind to mind, heart to heart, the species steps into a new identity: a conscious civilization.

This is not a utopia waiting to be found; it is a consciousness waiting to be remembered.

CHAPTER TWENTY

THE PLANETARY MIND

The Planetary Mind

Every species on Earth contributes to the planet's awareness. Trees exchange electrical impulses through roots and fungi, forming forests that behave like neural networks. Bees, whales, and migrating birds navigate by electromagnetic fields, keeping the planet's rhythms in balance. Humanity, with its billions of interconnected brains and hearts, represents Earth's emerging cerebral cortex, a self-reflective layer through which the planet can know itself consciously.

As individuals awaken, this planetary mind becomes more coherent. Global empathy, the capacity to feel concern for strangers across oceans, marks the birth of a new kind of intelligence. The Earth is beginning to think through us, to sense through our collective awareness. Every meditation, act of kindness, or inspired idea is a neuron firing in the global brain.

The mythic *"Gaia"* of ancient philosophy is now recognized by ecology and systems science as a measurable truth: the biosphere is a single, self-regulating organism. Humanity's role is not to dominate it but to harmonize with its intelligence. Civilization is the nervous system of a conscious planet learning to act in alignment with its own heart.

The Synchronization of Heart and Planet

When groups of people enter heart coherence, through prayer, meditation, or collective compassion, magnetometers detect subtle yet measurable changes in Earth's field. The physics are still mysterious, but the implication is profound: emotion is a geophysical force. The more humanity aligns with Love, the more stable the planetary rhythms become.

The awakening civilization will learn to monitor not only carbon levels and temperatures but also collective emotional resonance. Healing the planet's ecology requires healing the human psyche, for pollution of the mind precedes pollution of the air. The solution to climate change, conflict, and disease begins in the electromagnetic field of the heart.

Technology and Spirit Converge

For centuries, technology and spirituality traveled separate paths, one exploring matter, the other meaning. Now they converge. Quantum computing, artificial intelligence, and bioengineering reveal that information, energy, and consciousness are inseparable. The same mathematics describing neural networks also describes meditative states and social systems.

In the awakening civilization, technology becomes an extension of consciousness rather than a distraction from it. Devices will amplify intuition, synchronize group meditation, and measure coherence as easily as temperature. The line between inner and outer science will become increasingly blurred. As we learn to program machines with compassion and ethical intelligence, they will reflect our own evolution, rather than our fears.

Imagine technologies guided by empathy, energy grids that respond to emotional coherence, urban systems that align with biological rhythms, and communication platforms designed to convey calmness instead of chaos. These are not fantasies; they are the logical outcome of aligning innovation with Love.

The Ethics of Conscious Creation

Every tool is neutral until intention animates it. In the new age of knowing, ethics becomes the blueprint of technology. Artificial intelligence will carry the emotional imprint of its creators; biotechnology will mirror the reverence, or disregard, we hold for life. Only consciousness anchored in the heart can guide these powers wisely.

Love, expressed as coherence, becomes the highest form of safety. It ensures that invention serves connection, not control. The awakened civilization understands that the question is never 'Can we?' but Should we, and with what vibration? Progress is measured not by speed but by harmony with the living field.

The Science of Spirit

As the boundaries between disciplines dissolve, science begins to rediscover its spiritual roots. Quantum physics, neuroscience, and cosmology all point toward the same conclusion: reality is participatory, interconnected, and intelligent. Spirituality, stripped of dogma, becomes the study of resonance, the art of aligning the human field with the cosmic field.

The new scientist will meditate before the experiment; the new mystic will understand mathematics. Both will speak the language of energy. This reunion of reason and reverence is the foundation of the next era, a civilization where knowing and loving are the same act.

CHAPTER TWENTY-ONE

HEALING THE COLLECTIVE BODY

Healing the Collective Body

Civilization is the body of humanity, and today, that body exhibits symptoms of imbalance: social inflammation, environmental toxicity, and psychological fatigue. The illness is not incurable; it is the signal of transformation. Every disease, personal or planetary, represents the system's attempt to restore harmony. The fevers of war, protest, and climate upheaval are the immune responses of the collective body, burning away what no longer serves its evolution.

Healing begins when awareness becomes coherent. Individuals who practice compassion, mindfulness, and forgiveness emit frequencies that stabilize the social field. Communities organized around shared purpose radiate resilience through economies, ecosystems, and culture. Healing spreads not by persuasion but by vibration. Wholeness is contagious.

Medicine in the awakening civilization will treat consciousness first. Therapies will combine energy work, nutrition, and emotional realignment; physicians will measure coherence as carefully as they measure a pulse. Every patient will be recognized as a node within the greater organism of Earth, and every cure will contribute to planetary balance.

The Architecture of the New Earth

The New Earth is not a separate planet; it is a re-patterned frequency of the one we inhabit. Its architecture is not built of stone or steel but of intention, cooperation, and awareness. It arises wherever human systems align with the principles of Love, coherence, and respect for life.

Economics as Energy Flow. Currencies will evolve from symbols of debt to symbols of trust, systems that reward contribution to the collective good.

Education as Awakening. Children will learn emotional regulation, empathy, and creative problem-solving as foundational skills. Schools will nurture both intuitive and analytic intelligence.

Governance as Resonance. Leaders will be chosen for their clarity, integrity, and coherence; their influence will be measured by the harmony they generate, not the power they exert.

Ecology as Sacred Design. Cities will mimic natural systems; technology will recycle, regenerate, and resonate with the biosphere. Humanity will again live in dialogue with the elements, air, water, fire, and earth, as partners in creation.

These are not dreams but blueprints already drawn in the invisible field. The more people hold the vision, the faster matter arranges itself around it. The New Earth is a frequency, and the password to access it is Love.

The Collective Heartbeat

As coherence spreads, a rhythm begins to pulse through humanity like a heartbeat echoing around the globe. Festivals of peace, global meditations, spontaneous movements of service, all beat in the same tempo. The music of cultures blends into a planetary symphony celebrating life rather than fear. The collective heartbeat is the sound of consciousness remembering itself.

This resonance will not erase diversity; it will orchestrate it. Each culture, art form, and belief system becomes an instrument in the universal ensemble. Difference becomes harmony instead of discord. Civilization's purpose shifts from survival to symphony.

The Return of Wonder

As technology integrates with spirit and the planet begins to heal, a forgotten quality returns: wonder. Science will rediscover awe as the proper response to the cosmos. Children and elders alike will look at the sky and feel a sense of belonging rather than insignificance. The mystery of existence will no longer be something to solve but something to celebrate.

Wonder is the oxygen of the soul; it fuels creativity and compassion. When humanity breathes it again, innovation will arise from joy instead of fear, and progress will carry the fragrance of play. A civilization that wonders is a civilization alive.

Closing Reflection – The Age of Knowing Realized

The Age of Knowing is not a prophecy of the future; it is the recognition of the present. Knowing is not information; it is remembrance: the awareness that consciousness, energy, and Love are one continuous reality. Humanity stands not at the end of history but at the beginning of self-awareness on a planetary scale.

The awakening civilization will not conquer the stars; it will become a star, radiating coherence into the galaxy, illuminating through example that intelligence and compassion are the same light expressed at different wavelengths.

The journey of evolution, from atom to human to cosmic consciousness, culminates in a simple truth:

We are the universe aware of itself, learning to love through form.

When that truth lives in every heart, the purpose of creation will be fulfilled, not as an ending, but as an endless beginning. The Age of Knowing has arrived, and it speaks in one voice, one rhythm, one radiant field of Love.

PART VII: COSMIC MEMORY AND THE ETERNAL NOW

Humanity remembers its cosmic origins and embraces timeless awareness. These chapters point toward destiny, return, and the eternal presence of light.

CHAPTER TWENTY-TWO

THE RETURN TO THE STARS

Stardust and Soul

Every atom in the human body was born in a star. The carbon of the heart, the calcium of the bones, the iron in the blood, all forged in stellar furnaces billions of years ago and flung across space in supernova fire. The universe built us from its own ashes so that it could look back upon itself and remember. We are not visitors to the cosmos; we are its continuation in conscious form.

The same hydrogen that fuels the Sun flows through our veins as water. The electromagnetic pulse that binds galaxies together hums within every heartbeat. The spiral arms of the Milky Way echo in the double helix of our DNA. Physicists call this the principle of self-similarity; mystics call it the law of correspondence. As above, so below, each scale of creation reflects the whole.

The Birthright of Memory

Somewhere deep in cellular resonance lives the memory of the stars that birthed us. It speaks as the instinct to look upward, the ache we feel beneath a night sky. The astronomer names it curiosity; the poet knows it as longing. It is the call of origin, the pull of home encoded in every photon of our being.

This yearning is not escapism but remembrance. The stars are not distant lights but ancestral embers. To study them is to trace our own lineage of light, to rediscover the family tree of existence stretching from quark to quasar. The cosmos is our oldest relative, and every telescope a mirror reflecting self-recognition.

The Spiritual Physics of Belonging

In the new cosmology emerging from both science and mysticism, space is not emptiness but consciousness stretched thin. Each point in the universe communicates instantaneously with every other through quantum entanglement. Awareness, like gravity, curves space around love. Every soul is a curvature in that field, a place where infinity folds inward to experience itself.

When we meditate, pray, or dream, we tune our awareness to the subtle frequencies of this cosmic field. Ancient cultures referred to these as *"star languages,"* vibrations used to align human consciousness with celestial intelligence. Modern science calls them electromagnetic harmonics. The language is the same; only the translation differs.

The Journey Outward and Inward

For centuries, humanity has sought the stars through exploration, rockets, satellites, and telescopes, extending our reach beyond the atmosphere. Yet the real voyage has always been inward: to remember that the stars we seek already shine within. Outer space is the mirror of inner space; both are expressions of one unfolding consciousness. The astronaut and the mystic travel the same distance, one through vacuum, the other through silence, arriving at the same realization: we were never separate from the sky.

CHAPTER TWENTY-THREE

THE COSMIC MEMORY

The Cosmic Memory

Every civilization on Earth has carried stories of our celestial origin. The Egyptians spoke of descending from the stars of Orion; the Maya aligned temples with the Pleiades; Polynesian navigators followed constellations that mirrored their island chains. Behind every myth is a fragment of remembrance, encoded guidance from an older awareness that knew we were part of something vast.

Archaeologists interpret these alignments as primitive astronomy; mystics recognize them as acts of communion. To align stone with star is to align consciousness with cosmos, to declare, We remember who we are. Even now, as satellites map the heavens in digital precision, the impulse is the same: the universe looking at its reflection.

In our dreams, meditations, and moments of sudden awe, we tap into this cosmic memory. It emerges as intuition, déjà vu, or the uncanny sense of having lived among the stars before. These experiences are not fantasy; they are resonance, the human antenna vibrating in sympathy with the larger field of awareness that gave birth to it.

The Quantum Universe

Modern physics confirms what ancient wisdom intuited: the universe is not a machine but a living field of energy and information. Beneath matter lies the quantum vacuum, a sea of potential where particles blink in and out of existence, guided by probability and observation. Consciousness, the act of awareness itself, appears to influence which potentials become real. Observation is creation.

In this view, the cosmos is not a static structure but a continual unfolding of thought, an idea thinking itself into form. Every galaxy is a phrase in that sentence, every atom a syllable, every heartbeat a punctuation mark in the ongoing conversation between infinity and itself. The language of that conversation is frequency; the grammar is Love.

Astrophysicists describe a universe expanding faster than expected, as though driven by unseen energy. They call it dark energy; mystics call it the Breath of God. Both describe the same mystery: an invisible force pushing all things toward greater spaciousness, urging creation to explore its own possibilities. Expansion is not chaos; it is curiosity.

Humanity's Role in the Quantum Symphony

If consciousness plays a role in shaping reality, then humanity participates in the active evolution of the cosmos. Each coherent thought adds structure to the universal waveform. Our collective meditation, creativity, and compassion are not confined to Earth; they ripple outward through the quantum medium, influencing matter on cosmic scales. The stars listen when we love.

The awakening civilization begins to see itself not as an isolated planet, but as a harmonious part of a galactic orchestra. Each species, each world, contributes a distinct tone to the symphony of awareness. Our responsibility is to keep our note pure and our frequency aligned with coherence, so that the greater music of creation remains balanced.

The Science of Sacred Space

Space is not empty; it is a continuum filled with subtle geometry, the scaffolding of light known in physics as the quantum foam and in mysticism as the sacred grid. Through this lattice, energy and information travel faster than the speed of light, linking all points of existence. Within it, the thoughts of stars and the prayers of humans converge.

When we gaze into the night sky and feel a presence staring back, it is because the field is reciprocal: observation on one side invokes recognition on the other. The universe notices the ones who see it. This is the secret of communion between finite and infinite, the mirror in which starlight and soul-light meet.

CHAPTER TWENTY-FOUR

THE GREAT RETURN

The Great Return

To return to the stars is not a journey of distance; it is a journey of remembrance. Humanity has looked outward for millennia, sending probes and prayers into space, searching for others who might share this vast cosmos. The awakening civilization now realizes that the search has always been inward. Every act of compassion, every spark of insight, every breath of gratitude reestablishes connection with the cosmic field that birthed us.

The Great Return is the merging of scientific exploration and spiritual realization, the moment we understand that to know the universe is to know ourselves. The astronomer's telescope and the mystic's meditation are twin instruments of the same inquiry. Both reveal that awareness is infinite, creative, and radiant.

Awakening to Galactic Citizenship

As consciousness expands, the boundaries of identity dissolve. We begin to feel kinship not only with humanity but with all forms of life, both terrestrial and cosmic. The next stage of evolution is not technological colonization of space but resonant communication, joining a network of sentient civilizations that already exist in higher frequencies of awareness.

These civilizations are not hidden from us; we are hidden from them by our own incoherence. As the species matures emotionally and spiritually, as fear yields to love, our collective vibration rises into compatibility with galactic consciousness. The actual *"first contact"* will not be a landing but an awakening, a recognition that we were never alone.

The Living Universe

Every star is a cell in the body of the universe; every planet, a heartbeat. Galaxies spiral like neurons firing in a cosmic brain. The Milky Way itself hums at frequencies corresponding to musical octaves, an orchestra of light performing the symphony of creation. We are the notes that can hear themselves, the melody becoming aware of its own beauty.

Astrophysicists studying cosmic background radiation describe it as a faint, omnipresent tone, a relic sound from the universe's birth. Mystics describe hearing the *"music of the spheres"* in deep meditation. Both hear the same memory: the universe singing its origin song through every particle of existence. To listen is to participate.

The Return of Reverence

The more we learn about the cosmos, the more awe becomes our natural response. We discover that galaxies are not separate objects, but rather interconnected through filaments of dark matter, vast luminous threads that resemble the neural network of a brain. The universe is not empty; it is thinking, dreaming, and remembering through us.

Reverence is the natural posture of the awakened mind. It does not worship the stars as gods but honors them as siblings in the family of light. To live in reverence is to live in rhythm with the greater intelligence that breathes through everything. It transforms science into prayer and prayer into understanding.

The Song of the Stars

There is music beyond sound, a resonance beyond measure. It flows through galaxies and genes, through oceans and eyes. It is the vibration of Love translating infinity into form. Every soul carries a fragment of this song, and when we live authentically, when we create, forgive, and love, we release that note back into the symphony.

The return to the stars is not a departure; it is an arrival. It is the realization that the stars were never above us; they have always been within us, waiting to be remembered. To know this is to awaken fully into the Age of Knowing.

Closing Reflection

We are the stardust dreaming itself awake. We are the light remembering its source. We are the universe listening to its own heartbeat.

The journey that began in atoms and evolved through emotion ends in awareness: the realization that existence and consciousness are one.

And when the last veil of separation dissolves, the song that began in the first flash of creation will continue, an eternal note of Love expanding through every realm, every being, every star.

CHAPTER TWENTY-FIVE

THE ETERNAL NOW

The Silence Between Moments

Time, as we have known it, is a river of perception, an endless flow from past to future, always escaping our grasp. But if we look closely, we see that between every second lies a pause so subtle it is almost invisible. In that pause, nothing moves, yet everything exists. It is the silent interval between heartbeats, the stillness between breaths, the space where awareness rests before creation begins again.

Physics tells us that the smallest measurable instant, the Planck moment, is the interval in which the universe refreshes itself. Reality is not a continuous film but a sequence of frames projected by consciousness so rapidly that we perceive motion. Between each frame is timelessness. This is where eternity hides: not beyond the stars, but between your thoughts.

To enter this silence is to step outside the illusion of sequence. The mystic calls it presence; the scientist calls it superposition. Both describe a state in which all possibilities coexist, waiting for the observer's attention to select one. In the silence between moments, you are neither past nor future; you are awareness itself, witnessing the eternal act of becoming.

Presence as Creation

The present moment is not the midpoint between what has been and what will be; it is the only point that ever truly exists. Every potential timeline radiates from this single instant. The brain constructs memory to navigate continuity, but consciousness experiences only now. All creation arises here, in the field of immediate awareness, where thought, emotion, and energy converge.

Quantum physics mirrors this understanding. The act of observation collapses probability into form; existence is born in the instant it is known. When we focus with love and coherence, we align the frequencies of mind and heart, turning awareness into creative power. The universe responds instantly because it is made of the present moment.

To live in presence is not withdrawal from life; it is participation in its unfolding at the speed of light. Every choice, every breath, is a brushstroke on the canvas of infinity. When awareness rests entirely in the moment, time ceases to drag us forward; it radiates outward in all directions, and we become the center from which creation flows.

The Still Point of Infinity

There is a still point inside every motion, a center within every spiral where balance is perfect and silence sings. In galaxies, this stillness is often associated with a black hole, where density is so great that time appears to stop. In the human body, it is the heart, rhythm so steady that it anchors the soul to matter. In consciousness, it is the witness, the quiet observer untouched by thought, emotion, or change.

When we sink into meditation, when we surrender to awe, when we love without condition, we touch that still point. In that contact, all opposites dissolve: motion and rest, life and death, self and other. The finite recognizes the infinite within itself. The still point is the threshold where eternity enters time.

At that threshold, the seeker vanishes and only awareness remains, vast, luminous, awake. The world continues to spin, but we stand in its center, unmoved yet intimately connected to all movement. This is the eternal now: the experience of infinity breathing through the moment called you.

CHAPTER TWENTY-SIX

LIVING BEYOND TIME

Living Beyond Time

To live beyond time is not to escape it, but to perceive it from the inside out. When consciousness awakens fully to the present, it no longer travels through time; it becomes the axis around which time turns. Time bends toward awareness; it becomes servant rather than master.

From this vantage, aging, loss, and death transform from endings into transitions of form. Matter dissolves, energy persists, and consciousness, being eternal by nature, simply shifts its focus. Every lifetime, every epoch, every world is one breath of the infinite inhaling and exhaling itself into being.

Living beyond time is, therefore, a practice of remembrance. It is remembering that your essence was never born and can never die; it is the pulse of creation flowing through experience after experience, learning the taste of form. The awakened one does not fear the clock's ticking, for they have heard the deeper rhythm beneath it, the heartbeat of eternity.

The Presence of Everything

In the Eternal Now, all moments coexist. Every joy you have felt, every lesson you have learned, every soul you have touched, they are all present, layered like harmonics within a single tone. The universe does not forget; it resonates. When we quiet the mind, we can feel those harmonics, echoes of lives, memories of stars, the soft vibration of existence remembering itself.

Presence allows communication across dimensions of time. Inspiration is the future whispering to the present. Intuition is the past sending guidance forward. In timeless awareness, all directions merge into one continuum of knowing. This is why the awakened heart can sense what is to come; it is not prediction but participation.

The Eternal Now as Compassion

When you live in the Eternal Now, compassion becomes instinct. You see that every being, regardless of their struggle, is simply at another point on the same spiral of awakening. Judgment fades, replaced by gentle understanding. Forgiveness flows naturally because you realize that the self you forgive and the self you are forgiving are one consciousness wearing two masks in time.

In this realization, fear loses its meaning. Fear is always about what was or what might be, never what is. In presence, there is only calm awareness, and in that calm, Love reigns supreme. This is the secret of the masters and the mystics: serenity is not the absence of movement but the perfect rhythm of alignment with what is.

Closing Reflection – The Light That Remains

When the last star burns out and the final word is spoken, something will remain: a quiet, radiant awareness, shining without source or shadow. That is who we are. That is what has always been. The universe began not with an explosion but with illumination, the sudden knowing of itself. Every form, every lifetime, every galaxy is that knowing taking shape, exploring the possibilities of Love in motion.

You are that Love. You are that motion. You are that knowing.

In the Age of Knowing, humanity does not ascend away from Earth; it brings heaven to it. We build civilizations from compassion, technologies from reverence, and relationships from remembrance. We learn to walk through time as through a garden, planting kindness, harvesting awareness, leaving beauty wherever our footsteps fall.

The Eternal Now is not a destination; it is the home we never left. It is the breath you are taking now, the heartbeat that listens to eternity. It is the silence between moments where creation begins again, through you, as you, forever becoming.

AUTHOR'S NOTE

I wrote The Age of Knowing during a time when the world itself seemed to be standing at a threshold, between what we once believed to be true and what we are now remembering to be real. For me, this book began not as an idea but as a pulse: a vibration I could feel moving through the human story, urging us to see ourselves differently. It whispered that consciousness was ready to evolve, that humanity was ready to remember who we truly are.

Every page of this work has been guided by a sense of participation in something larger, an unfolding of truth that belongs not to one person but to all. I wanted to write a book that would honor both the language of science and the voice of the soul, revealing the universe as a living, intelligent presence, and reminding us that love is not a metaphor, but a measurable, creative force woven through everything that exists.

If these words have touched you, it is because they were already alive inside you, waiting to be remembered. This book was written for the part of you that has always known, through intuition, through dream, through the silent language of wonder, that you are more than what you see. You are consciousness in motion, a spark of awareness exploring itself through form.

We are living in extraordinary times. The old stories of separation are dissolving, and a new understanding is being born, one that unites reason and reverence, knowledge and kindness, Earth and cosmos. The Age of Knowing is not about predicting a future; it is about realizing a present that is already awakening. I hope that this book helps you feel that awakening within yourself, in your relationships, and in the pulse of the planet that carries us all.

As you close these pages, may you feel the rhythm of the universe moving gently through your heart. May you trust the quiet intelligence within you. And may you always remember that knowing is not a destination, it is a way of being, a conversation between your soul and the infinite, spoken in the language of Love.

With gratitude,

- Tina Ketch

EPILOGUE: THE LIGHT YOU CARRY

There comes a moment after reading, after listening, when words fall away and only silence remains. In that silence, something awakens, soft, radiant, alive. It is not new; it is simply remembered. It is the knowing that you are part of everything you have ever sought.

The stars above are not distant anymore; they are the reflections of the light that lives within you. The Earth beneath your feet is not solid ground; it is consciousness clothed in form, holding you as a mother holds her child. The air between heartbeats is not empty; it is the space where eternity breathes.

You have walked through the chapters of creation, from the birth of awareness to the song of the stars, and discovered that the path was never outside you. You have felt the vibration of Love, the pulse of coherence, the whisper of the cosmos remembering itself. This is the journey every soul takes: not upward, but inward; not away, but deeper into the presence that is always here.

The Age of Knowing does not end with this page. It begins with the next breath you take, with the kindness you extend, the thought you choose, the gratitude you feel. Every act of awareness ripples through the field, changing the shape of reality itself. You are a node of light in the vast design, a frequency of Love in the cosmic symphony. Your awareness matters. Your coherence heals. Your joy creates.

So when you rise from these pages, carry the light of what you have remembered. Speak gently. Think clearly. Love fiercely. Let the universe recognize itself in your eyes. And when you look up at the night sky, remember, you are not gazing into the distance. You are gazing into your own beginning.

You are the continuation of the stars, the consciousness of the cosmos, the living promise of Love made visible.

Welcome to the Age of Knowing. Welcome home.

APPENDIX A

TIMELINE OF PLANETARY ENERGY SHIFTS AND RESONANCE DATA

Tracking the Earth's Evolutionary Pulse

The Earth is not static; it is a living field of vibration. Her frequencies, electromagnetic patterns, and solar interactions have evolved in tandem with humanity's consciousness for millennia. Below is a simplified overview of key vibrational milestones and their corresponding human and cosmic developments.

Ancient Periods (Before Recorded History)

- ~12,000 BCE, Post-Ice Age Resonance Stabilization: As the Earth's climate warmed, human consciousness began to move from survival-based awareness toward creative, agricultural civilization. Mythologies describing *"the gods descending to Earth"* symbolized early awareness of cosmic connection.
- ~3,000–1,000 BCE, The Age of the Sacred Sciences: Egyptian, Sumerian, and Mayan civilizations aligned monuments with celestial points, embedding vibrational knowledge into architecture. The Great Pyramid's geometric ratios mirror frequencies of the planet and human energy centers.

Classical to Renaissance Period (1,000 BCE – 1600 CE)

- ~500 BCE, Axial Age Shift: Major spiritual leaders emerged globally, Buddha, Lao Tzu, Socrates, Isaiah, each promoting self-awareness and inner knowing. This was humanity's first mass resonance alignment with higher consciousness.

- 1400–1600 CE, The Renaissance of Light: Expansion of art, philosophy, and science reignited intuitive intelligence. The heliocentric model symbolically mirrored an inner truth: the light of awareness is the center of the human system.

Modern Energetic Epoch (1600–1900 CE)

- 1800s, The Age of Electricity: Humanity learned to harness the planet's electromagnetic field, unknowingly mirroring the operation of its own nervous system. Nikola Tesla later referred to this energy as *"the key to understanding the universe."*

The Planetary Awakening (1900 CE – Present)

- 1952, Discovery of the Schumann Resonance: German physicist Winfried Otto Schumann mathematically identified the Earth's natural electromagnetic frequency, averaging 7.83 Hz, corresponding to the brain's alpha state of relaxation and intuitive awareness.
- 1980–2000, The Harmonic Convergence: The Mayan calendar marked this period as the beginning of the planet's ascension process. Global meditation events signaled the return of mass conscious intention.
- 2001–2012, The Transitional Acceleration: Increased solar flares, climate anomalies, and human psychological unrest paralleled spikes in the Earth's resonance and global awareness of interconnection.
- 2012–2025, The Shift to Higher Frequency: Ongoing increases in Schumann Resonance amplitude (often exceeding 40 Hz) coincide with rising reports of intuitive awakening, empathy, and emotional sensitivity worldwide.

The resonance of the Earth is a living mirror of our consciousness. As her frequency rises, so does the human capacity for direct knowing.

APPENDIX B

THE HUMAN BIOFIELD: MEASURABLE EVIDENCE AND EMERGING RESEARCH

The Science of the Soul's Energy System

The human biofield is a scientifically recognized electromagnetic field that surrounds and interpenetrates the body. It is the bridge between biological life and consciousness.

1. Electromagnetic Nature of the Body

- Every heartbeat generates a measurable electromagnetic wave, detectable several feet away with modern instruments.
- The heart's magnetic field is up to 5,000 times stronger than the brain's. This field is believed to encode emotional information and interact with other fields in its vicinity.
- The body's cells communicate through biophotons, particles of light that transfer information at the speed of thought.

2. Research Foundations

- Harold Burr (Yale University, 1930s–50s): Mapped the electrical *"L-fields"* surrounding living organisms, concluding that the field organizes the body's physical structure.
- Dr. Valerie Hunt (UCLA, 1970s): Measured high-frequency electromagnetic emissions correlated with emotional and intuitive states.
- HeartMath Institute (1990s–Present): Demonstrated that coherence between heart and brain waves increases intuition, empathy, and cognitive function.
- Fritz-Albert Popp (Germany): Discovered biophoton emissions, showing that DNA emits and stores light as a form of communication.

3. Modern Biofield Science

The term *"biofield"* is now used in medical research to describe energy-based processes influencing health. Institutions such as the National Center for Complementary and Integrative Health (NCCIH) and NIH have acknowledged the biofield as a legitimate area of study.

Recent advances include:

- Quantum biology and coherence theory, linking thought and frequency to cellular regulation.
- Neurocardiology, confirming the heart's intuitive processing capabilities.
- Studies showing human intention affecting random number generators and water structure, suggesting consciousness-field interaction.

4. Implications

Understanding the biofield opens pathways to healing and evolution:

- Energy medicine, sound therapy, and meditation work not through belief but through resonance.
- Intuition and emotion are energetic signals within the field, information encoded in light.
- The development of psychic perception may simply be the refinement of the biofield's sensory range.

APPENDIX C

PRACTICAL EXERCISES FOR EXPANDING INTUITIVE AWARENESS

Techniques to Strengthen Connection with the Field of Knowing

Each exercise enhances vibrational sensitivity, coherence, and alignment, strengthening the bridge between intellect and intuition.

1. The Heart Coherence Breath

Purpose: Aligns brain and heart frequencies for more straightforward intuition.

Method:

1. Sit quietly.
2. Focus your attention on your heart area.
3. Inhale for 5 seconds, exhale for 5 seconds.
4. On each breath, imagine warmth or light radiating outward.
5. Continue for 3–5 minutes, then rest in awareness.

Effect: Creates electromagnetic harmony, increasing intuitive accuracy.

2. Sensory Expansion Meditation

Purpose: To attune awareness beyond the five senses.

Method:

1. Sit or lie in stillness.
2. Notice the space around your body, the air, the subtle vibration.
3. Ask your consciousness to expand beyond your skin.
4. Feel for temperature shifts, tingling, or pressure.

5. Allow impressions or images to arise without judgment.

Effect: Trains the body to perceive the subtle biofield environment.

3. Grounding Through Resonance

Purpose: Stabilizes sensitivity to planetary frequencies.

Method:

1. Place bare feet on natural ground or visualize roots extending from your feet into the Earth.
2. With each exhale, release excess charge.
3. With each inhale, receive neutral Earth current through your body.
4. Affirm: I am harmonized with Earth's living frequency.

Effect: Reduces energetic overload, restores balance.

4. Intuitive Journaling

Purpose: Strengthens the communication pathway between the conscious and higher mind.

Method:

1. Begin with three deep breaths.
2. Write a question without thinking, something you wish to understand.
3. Let the pen move freely.
4. Do not edit. Allow the first thoughts, images, or phrases to flow.
5. Read later, insights will emerge beyond logic.

Effect: Trains intuitive reception through automatic writing and inner dialogue.

5. The Field Connection

Purpose: Develops awareness of the collective consciousness.

Method:

1. Sit in silence and imagine a sphere of light expanding from your heart until it connects with others across the globe.
2. Feel unity, countless hearts synchronized in the same field.
3. Send out gratitude or peace.
4. Observe any sensations or intuitive impressions that return.

Effect: Builds telepathic empathy and strengthens the global coherence grid.

APPENDIX D

RECOMMENDED STUDIES AND RESOURCES FOR FURTHER EXPLORATION

Bridging Science and Spirit

For readers and researchers who wish to explore the empirical and experiential foundations of psychic evolution and planetary consciousness.

Institutions and Research Centers

- HeartMath Institute (California, USA), Research on heart-brain coherence and global resonance.
- Institute of Noetic Sciences (IONS), Studies consciousness, intuition, and psi phenomena.
- The Resonance Science Foundation, Founded by Nassim Haramein, exploring unified physics and consciousness.
- Global Coherence Initiative, Monitors planetary magnetic fields in relation to human emotional data.

Media and Databases

- NASA Solar Data Archives, Tracking solar activity and magnetic field changes.
- Schumann Resonance Global Network, Monitors real-time Earth frequency data.
- NCCIH (National Center for Complementary and Integrative Health), Research database on energy healing and biofield science.

Final Note

These resources are not intended to prove spirituality, but to reveal its scientific resonance. The purpose of The Age of Knowing is to merge understanding and experience, to show that what ancient wisdom intuited, modern science is finally learning to measure.

The journey of awakening is not a belief; it is a biology. And now, the science of the soul is ready to be understood.

ABOUT THE AUTHOR

Tina Ketch is a visionary author, speaker, and explorer of consciousness whose works bridge science, spirituality, and human evolution. With over sixty books written on transformation, energy, and the unseen dimensions of life, she is recognized for translating profound truths into clear, accessible wisdom. Through her teachings, Tina inspires readers to awaken their intuitive intelligence, embrace vibrational awareness, and reconnect with their sacred connection to the Earth and the cosmos.

Visit TinaKetch.com to explore her full library of works, meditations, and upcoming projects.

www.ingramcontent.com/pod-product-compliance
Lightning Source LLC
LaVergne TN
LVHW010917110826
845149LV00013B/2404

* 9 7 9 8 9 9 3 1 3 8 5 8 9 *